PRAISE FOR TEAM BEING

"To paraphrase Spock, 'The power of the r̶ the few . . . or the one.' This is the message engaging road map through a journey from t̶ ᴜɪtary professional confinement to the joys of creativ̶ ̶e collaboration and the resulting rewards: profound success and ̶ greater personal fulfill-ment. Having worked as a writer and co-executive producer in prime-time television and a producer and executive in television news, I can tell you that teamwork is more than a take-it-or-leave-it thing that could be useful . . . teamwork is everything. *Team Being* is a must-read and recipe for success in not just creative fields, but any field."—**Jon Greene**, Emmy Award–winning screenwriter; writer and co-executive producer, NBC's *Law & Order: Special Victims Unit*

"Rarely a book comes along that casts a light on that intangible 'something' that you know has been missing from every book you've ever read on a subject, and *Team Being* does just that for the subject of teamwork. Focusing on the real challenges undergirding teams and collaboration, such as chaos, conflict, risk, and abrasion, the authors focus on the surprising way these each benefit the process of collaboration. Engaging and thought-provoking, this work thoughtfully dissects the mixed human attributes and emotions that lead to individuals engaging successfully in teamwork."—**Kelly Leahy Whitney**, Ed.D., chief product & partnerships officer iCivics, Inc.—founded in 2008 by retired Supreme Court of the United States Justice Sandra Day O'Connor

"As an active Hollywood TV and film producer, I spend my days collaborat-ing with some of the most brilliant creatives on Earth. But with great minds come great discrepancies in thought, ego, and sense of self—all traits that can derail a project, turning your next Oscar or Emmy winner into a muddy, unwatchable embarrassment. At the very heart of this risk is teamwork—or lack thereof. I'm thankful that Gary and Michael put together such a well-researched exploration into what it means to be an effective collaborator, using easily digestible, real-world stories backed up by compelling science. The lessons learned in this book will help you—like it did me—in any collaboration, whether you're making a movie; working on a team project; or just trying to negotiate your complicated family life. If you like getting the most out of yourself and those around you, *Team Being* is an investment that will pay off creatively, emotionally, and financially many times over. I can't recommend it enough."—**Corey Marsh**, executive vice president and producer, Wonderland Sound and Vision

"Decades of experience in fostering and studying teamwork and creative collaboration are evident in every page of *Team Being*. Gemmill and Schoonmaker employ real-world examples and an expansive array of illustrations from across disciplines as they compose a compelling case for taking a holistic approach to cultivating this crucially important element of effectiveness for organizations of all types in an increasingly diverse and increasingly complex world."—**Nancy Cantor**, chancellor, Rutgers University–Newark

"Having a solid team is crucial. One of the many things I have learned from working at Microsoft and Xbox for the past 18 years: Your team work makes the dream work. Teamwork is not just a buzzword or aspiration. It's an absolute necessity for success in the modern workplace. When a well-tuned team comes together, you can create unimaginable energy and magic. In this book, Gary and Michael talk about the importance of teamwork and give multiple examples that should spark your imagination and motivate you to assemble a great team where you can create your own magic."—**Larry Hryb**, director of programming, Microsoft Gaming Network: Xbox Live

"Rarely is the term *metamorphosis* used to describe the evolution of team dynamics in the workplace. In the book *Team Being*, Gemmill and Schoonmaker re-imagine the power of creative collaboration in the future of work ecosystem by offering a future-forward roadmap for fueling a creative, agile and inclusive approach to organizational transformation. Gemmill and Schoonmaker examine the intricacies of individuals and their unique contribution to a powerful, meaningful and inclusive team experience, reinforcing that premise that differences, inclusion and belonging are critical accelerators to effectively leveraging the collective talent that exists in all organizations."—**Michelle Jones-Johnson**, vice president, talent and inclusion, chief diversity officer, WPI; president and founder, UnVeiled Leadership Consulting

"*Team Being* provides astounding and much-needed insight into two of the most significant issues in our contemporary culture. Across today's hyperconnected economy, leaders bemoan a growing lack of face-to-face engagement and emotional connectedness, while others struggle with growing beyond established experiences and interpretations. The authors expertly draw on decades of experiential research to both identify the underlying dynamics and issues, as well as develop a culture centered on creative collaboration and teamwork, across virtually any organization or group."—**Bob Kalka**, global vice president of cybersecurity, IBM

"Whether you're new to the workforce and looking for tips, or a seasoned professional striving to improve effectiveness, this book should be in your toolkit. Communication and collaboration are simple in concept, but often difficult in execution. If you're looking to learn and improve through understanding, this book is key. Gemmill and Schoonmaker spent years unlocking the art and science behind effective collaboration. The result is surprising, informative, and will no doubt make you a stronger professional."
—**Kate Martin**, project manager, Title Operations Innovation, Netflix

"This is an interesting and different way to look at teams that completely debunks conventional thinking. The authors explore the paradoxes and complexities of team life rather than propose a set of (too) simple how to-s and whys. They recognize the inherent need for individuals to acknowledge their singularity and to focus on team, and to do it at the same time. So instead of the oft used motto "there is no I in team," they suggest an "and" focus; an inside focus on self and an outside focus on collaboration. Simple and brilliant, and as they would say, not so easy to do."—**Gary Wagenheim**, PhD, international consultant and adjunct professor in management and organization studies, Beedie School of Business at Simon Fraser University in Vancouver, CA

"A thought-provoking book that delivers profound, new insights into the world of creative collaboration. This book clearly provides leaders with a road map for success that is pragmatic and applicable in any work setting. Gary and Michael have combined their deep expertise and talent to create a book that will develop and expand the readers understanding of creative collaboration and the complex forces at work in a collective setting."
—**Colleen L. Bielitz**, PhD, vice president of strategic initiatives and outreach, Southern Connecticut State University

"Currently most organizations, their managers/executives and individuals face uncertainties associated with substantial challenges—which upset the status quo. This book looks at an ingenious approach employing 'creative collaboration' to cope with such challenges. The authors' diverse backgrounds enrich the possibilities associated with this approach."
—**Mark Doctoroff**, PhD, international consultant and entrepreneur

Team Being

The Art and Science of Working Well with Others

Gary Gemmill
Michael Schoonmaker

ROWMAN & LITTLEFIELD
Lanham • Boulder • New York • London

Published by Rowman & Littlefield
An imprint of The Rowman & Littlefield Publishing Group, Inc.
4501 Forbes Boulevard, Suite 200, Lanham, Maryland 20706
www.rowman.com

6 Tinworth Street, London SE11 5AL

British Library Cataloguing in Publication Information Available

Library of Congress Cataloging-in-Publication Data

Library of Congress Control Number:2019951016
ISBN 978-1-4758-4984-4 (cloth : alk. paper)
ISBN 978-1-4758-4985-1 (paper : alk. paper)
ISBN 978-1-4758-4986-8 (electronic)

Contents

Contents

Preface

Team Being is about creative collaboration—what it is, how it works in actual practice, and how to maximize chances of doing it well. It is built on years of experience working with hundreds of nascent teams from education, business, and government, where participants were expected to generate results in collaborative formations of two to twenty-five people.

THE COLLABORATORS BEHIND TEAM BEING

There are two voices in collaboration behind this book. Our research and writing process is inductive: We start by working with and observing creative teams make their class projects. After class, we meet to talk about what happened, document it, and make sense of it. This is the nature of building understanding with grounded theory.

We have structured our writing as a conversation with readers, as if they are in the room with us, sharing perspectives on the practice of creative collaboration.

MICHAEL SCHOONMAKER

I come from the *creative side* of creative collaboration. I went to school in the early 1980s to learn how to produce television and film, and that is what I did in the industry. I worked at MTV when they played music videos, and then moved to the Olympic games at NBC. After that, I had the opportunity to return to my alma mater to teach creative visual storytelling to teams of aspiring television and film creators, and I have continued to do so for the past thirty years. Gary and I met in 1984, when I enrolled in a class he taught at the business school called Task Group Dynamics.

Gary was a leading figure in the field of organizational management, and his team dynamics classes were the subject of great lore around the university. What always amazed me was his uncanny ability to remain poised while the teams he coached worked through their various and often-explosive vulnerabilities as they struggled to work together. His quiet, encouraging, and even-tempered presence always encouraged his students to push on through the challenges in working together. His warm smile and peaceful eyes made students feel like they were going to be OK in the end. We referred to him as "Cool Hand Gary" for his poise in the presence of turmoil.

Years later, when I returned to the university to teach, I was thrilled to run into Gary unexpectedly on campus. He had retired from the full-time faculty but was still teaching teamwork classes in the MBA program. Teaching teamwork was an ever-rewarding habit he couldn't kick.

Before we parted ways, I asked him if he might be interested in visiting one of my large-group TV production classes to give me some pointers on how I might get them to work more effectively with each other. Even though Gary's work had been more focused on collaboration in business environments, I thought it would be very interesting to get his perspective on team dynamics in a creative and artistic setting. Gary happily agreed, and we have been working together since.

GARY GEMMILL

I was very thrilled when Michael and I crossed paths years after he was one of my students. When I observed the film and TV production teams and what they were doing, my heart jumped leaps and bounds. The artistic side of me was reawakened, and I wanted to be involved in working with these teams. One of my first experiences was with a film team that was making a short film involving the characters of an older man and a young woman. One of the students asked me if I would be willing to play the role of the older man. I indicated that I had not done any acting since I did some summer stock when I was an undergraduate, but I would be willing to give it a shot. From there, I was not just an actor but also an active participant-observer, gaining great insights into the team dynamics of a film and TV production team, from preproduction to final screening. What an eye-opener it was for me! I had no idea of the complexities involved in making a film or TV series. Clearly, the process in all the stages involved complex teamwork of the first order to deliver a meaningful film.

Previously, I spent most of my life researching and writing about the psychodynamics of leadership and small-group behavior. I coauthored two books: one deals with the psychodynamics of teams, and the other deals with the psychodynamics of personal development. I also published several articles in refereed journals on the psychodynamics of leadership and small-group behavior, including transformation processes, gender dynamics, dysfunctional dynamics, and the psychodynamics of intergroup behavior.

Much of my previous research and theory was based on working with executives and managers in work settings and students who were pursuing MBAs or PhDs in organizational behavior. My approach to both consulting on teamwork and teaching has always been experiential: I create structured experiential learning situations that engage and allow students to go deeper into the real dynamics involved in working with others. Stated somewhat differently, my hope is to provide a constructive mirror for them to examine and critically evaluate their actual behaviors in collaborative settings. Many of the structured experiential learning situations I use are ones that I have created and published.

Michael and I encourage readers to deepen their understanding of the forces involved in creative collaboration not only by reading our book, but also accessing readings like those we provide at the end of each chapter. References are listed so you can both explore subjects we cover further and also check us on our conclusions.

CREDIBILITY AND IDENTITY

As authors of this book, we believe the credibility of our findings depend on an honest and critical reflection of our identities. On the surface we can both be fairly described as a couple of "old white guys": upper middle class, cisgender, straight, nondisabled males. We're both PhDs and full professors in our fields who have enjoyed long and prosperous careers at a major R1 university. And if there is one thing we've learned about the value of such characteristics and accomplishments as they relate to research and teaching, it is that they are as much weaknesses as they are strengths. Unchecked privilege and position can easily blind one when it comes to contributing knowledge to the fields of practice. And on top of this, teamwork is an extremely dynamic process, often defying simple explanations and reductive steps.

This is why we have built our research on experiences and insights derived from complex human interaction, involving people from extraordinarily diverse walks of life in terms of social position, gender, race, ethnicity, and age, eclectically sprinkled with wide-ranging sets of values, ethics, and talents.

Because of this, our work is informed by an immensely humbling spectrum of challenges, surprises, and failures, which cultivate a thick skin and critical perspective on the practice of collaboration. We learned from our successes, but even more from our failures. And though we can say that tactics and insights of this book can and will lead to success, it is very important to realize that they do not eliminate the possibility of failure in specific situations. That is simply the nature of *Team Being*.

Introduction

Watching a process over and over can teach you a lot about it. That is what research is at its heart: systematic observation in search of patterns, behaviors, and outcomes. But can we ever completely figure out what we are examining if we observe it long enough? When it comes to teamwork, the answer is simple and certain: no, not completely.

But the *complicated* answer is more positive: Teamwork may resist simple and predictable explanation, but leaders can consistently succeed with teams if they thoughtfully consider and understand the forces at work in collaborative environments before applying them to their unique work settings. We share these complex insights by carefully examining and making sense of the primal forces at work (and play) in highly functioning creative teams. The more aware leaders are of these forces, the more empowered they are in team success; they are more able to lead teams by influence rather than blind authority.

We deconstruct the intricacies of the complex forces at work in team relations and exercise tactics to harness them for success. Learning how to work well with others is an inconvenience, not unlike grammar is to writing—we absolutely need it, but there is currently no natural, convenient, or effective place to learn it in organized education.

TEAM BEING

The title of this book, along with its approach to the subject of teamwork, is both a verb and a noun:

Verb: acting with maximum effectiveness in coordination with others toward a shared goal.

Noun: an individual distinguished from others by superior awareness and understanding of forces at play in collaborative environments.

This semantic perspective is used to call attention to the often-misunderstood and underappreciated complexities involved in teamwork. In most everyday teamwork situations, it is easier to stick to the simple surface of common-sense notions of working together.

You can find volumes of books about teamwork in libraries and stores that boil down its practice to a manageable few steps. There are considerably fewer books that delve beneath the surface of teamwork to its often-chaotic undercurrents like this book does.

FORCES

Our focus is on the invisible, dynamic, and often-unpredictable forces under the surface of most team environments. These forces cause individuals to be pushed or pulled in directions outside their individual control. And they don't conform to the commonsense or ideological codes of individual interaction.

Forces of creative collaboration are hard to explain in simple how-to terms because they are often unpredictable and difficult to replicate in all team situations. This is why this book focuses on understanding these forces—largely outside of awareness—before navigating them when leading and managing creative teams. In doing this, we borrow from lenses ranging from the astrophysical to the quantum in understanding dynamics in collaborative environments. We believe that this approach is more helpful in developing resilient understandings that can be applied to unique collaborative challenges in many areas of work that leaders and team members face on a daily basis. We embark on this method (as opposed to the "top ten steps to perfect teamwork") in order to get beyond the "how-to" to the "why" behind effective collaboration.

In the end, our experience over a five-year span of study indicates team leaders and team members must stumble through the helter-skelter of their particular team settings and members, all in the dense fog of dynamics surrounding team relations. The more leaders understand forces around teamwork, the better they can respond to the unique needs of their teams. There are no hidden messages or magical interventions, and yes, it is difficult work.

TERMS, ASSUMPTIONS, AND APPROACH TO CREATIVE COLLABORATION

We approach the practices of teamwork and collaboration in a complex manner, so it is important to be clear on our terms and assumptions around them. We use the words *teamwork* and *collaboration* interchangeably, even though others may sometimes use them differently. For instance, some may call an arbitrary or serially arranged group of individuals a team. When we use the word *team*, we are referring to a collection of individuals who share a common goal, who participate in collective activities with constructive intent, and who put collective interests and goals ahead of their own. Beyond this, there is little else that can be assumed, as every team, its context, and its individual members and power dynamics are unique. These unique factors can be understood, dealt with, and channeled toward team objectives through time, repeated interaction, and constructive feedback.

We interweave the concept of *creative* in our approach to understanding teamwork first because our research focused on creative teams—film and television story teams—and understanding the dynamics at play in their collective creative process. Creativity tends to have a complex connotation that involves transcending past and present situations and knowledge to create new and original ideas, forms, methods, interpretations, and solutions.

Former president of Pixar and Walt Disney Animation Studios Ed Catmull boils creativity down to simple terms: "It's problem solving, and problem solving means you've got something, you don't know what to do, so thinking that through is a creative act." Creativity tends to be thought of as solo act reduced to a single idea, when in reality, Catmull explains, "creativity involves a large number of people from different disciplines working effectively together to solve a great many problems."[1]

In addition to the observational context of our research, we see teamwork and creativity as complementary and largely bound together in most collaborative contexts. A creative team is a team with a clear, shared objective that is speculative, often from "scratch," original, and facing a constant risk of failure. When a creative team reaches its objective, something is created that did not exist before their collaborative venture. In our view, stoking collaborative work and objectives with the expectation of creative outcomes increases the complexity of team dynamics.

Creativity and complexity are not only on the rise across the world, but they are also seen as increasingly necessary skill sets of future leaders. In

2010, IBM's Institute for Business Value commissioned a study of 1,541 business leaders across the world and their thoughts on responding to a competitive and economic environment unlike anything that has come before.

They identify a rapid escalation of "complexity" as the biggest challenge confronting them and agree that it will accelerate in the future. They also identify "creativity" as the single most important leadership competency for enterprises seeking a path through this complexity. IBM CEO Samuel J. Palmisano summarizes,

> What we heard through the course of these in-depth discussions . . . is that events, threats and opportunities aren't just coming at us faster or with less predictability; they are converging and influencing each other to create entirely unique situations. These firsts-of-their-kind developments require unprecedented degrees of creativity—which has become a more important leadership quality than attributes like management discipline, rigor or operational acumen.[2]

OUR APPROACH TO THE STUDY AND PRACTICE OF CREATIVE COLLABORATION

In imparting what we believe to be best practices for leaders of creative teams, we focus on examining, interpreting, and better understanding the complex forces at work in collaborative settings. We do this instead of reducing what we see to simple, repetitive steps.

Our intended outcome is to provide readers an understanding of the complex forces surrounding collaborative work that can be coupled with expertise in their particular areas of practice and relationships with colleagues. We believe this complexity-empowered authorship is the best formula for success in creative collaboration.

It is important to recognize that teamwork does not function in a vacuum. It depends on and interacts with other variables, from office politics to unique personalities to unexpected problems, and team failure is an everyday possibility in all teams. This is why developing a complex framework of understanding can be more helpful than a simple one.

Theoretical physicist David Bohm developed a branch of quantum theory based on this notion: "I think we have to free our mind from the idea that order is always just some simple thing that we can grasp. Chaos is a kind of order."[3] Examining the often-chaotic elements involved in collaboration instead of looking away allows for the emergence of an entirely different perspective than we are accustomed to in individual environments.

Our findings are grounded in observations of and interactions with nascent creative teams working together for the first time toward a shared creative goal (mostly short films, TV productions, and public presentations). Continually observing the transformation from individual to collective states of mind allowed us to more clearly make sense of the relationship between behaviors and results. But these lessons are equally valuable for veteran teams as they are for newly assembled teams.

The teams we observed were not performing for research purposes; rather for educational outcomes in classes involving creative outcomes. As opposed to most academic project settings, we did discuss and provide a basic "roadmap of best practices" for students to consider as they worked together. Most but not all subjects of our observations were domestic and international college-age students. We used findings from our daily observations of their creative work to inform our analysis of complex forces in collaborative settings.

The insights we share with readers are grounded in "doing" creative collaboration. According to an oft-cited Chinese proverb, there is no substitute for true understanding of a practice:

> I hear and I forget
> I see and I remember
> I do and I understand

To maximize understanding in our study, we engaged in repetition to build and fortify our working theories on creative collaboration. We observed creative collaboration practices in action and then used additional observations to clarify, intensify, and readjust our understanding of collaborative dynamics to share with others.

We fortified our empirical findings with insights from hundreds of studies and perspectives on collaboration and allied fields. This broad collection of literature covers a vast range of topics, including chaos and quantum theory, complexity theory, social psychology, psychotherapy, unconscious behavior, sociology, anthropology, neuroscience, neurobiology, organizational behavior, leadership, small-group behavior, innovative management, economics, interpersonal behavior, public administration, hospital administration, medical science, and project management.

In the following pages, we use this research to help make sense of the forces and undercurrent of collaboration in creative teams: the good, the bad, and the ugly. Even as we publish this book, our understanding continues to grow. Such is the nature of complex processes: they never stop evolving, they do not just become static one day, and they most certainly never get easy.

Though we derive most of our findings from creative storytelling settings, we have found them to be relevant to any collaborative settings with objectives that require the effective coming together of multiple skills and talents. Perhaps the most unique aspect from this empirical setting was our continual supply of nascent teams and the transformation of individual mindsets (preconditioned "heroes") to collective mind-sets. This offered us not only the opportunity to collect reliable findings through repetitive study, but also the opportunity to explore novel approaches to collaborative practice.

READERS FOR WHOM WE HAVE WRITTEN THIS BOOK

A typical reader of this book is someone who is involved in establishing, developing, and leading teams to meet challenging objectives. Such a reader would likely encourage members of their teams to also read this book as a shared resource in their collective development. More specific areas of application include:

- Education (primary, secondary, and higher); ranging from teachers working on curriculum to principals to superintendents solving problems to school boards setting policies
- Engineering
- Entrepreneurship
- Leadership and management in all areas of business, from banking to retail
- Manufacturing
- Media, film, and TV studies; empowering young artists to exponentially build their creative power by working well with others
- Medicine
- Military
- Nonprofits and NGOs
- Project management
- Public and governmental administration
- Research and development; new product or new venture development
- Self-help; building leadership skills

Team Being is designed to provide a flexible map of collaboration dynamics to apply to unique work cultures, environments, and challenges.

THE STARTING POINT FOR *TEAM BEING*

We begin by considering the individual who enters a collaborative space. In the beginning of every team, there are individual human beings. Individual human beings do not immediately transform into team beings simply by being placed in a team. They enter a process of potential transformation.

Part I, "Singularity" examines the "I" in teams and takes on the questions that rise up from this transformation from individual human being to team being. Who is in the room? What are they about? What are they bringing in with them? This invites a conversation on the unconscious human factors of individual identity that arrive in the room but cannot be seen. Becoming aware of these unconscious forces is vital to the success of creative collaboration.

Part I

Singularity

Teamwork is essentially a plural endeavor. Take the commonly accepted adage, "There is no *I* in *team*. This suggests that, when "one" enters a collective environment, "one" automatically becomes "team." Whatever we were before the team is cast aside and forgotten. Let's just suddenly take on an entirely different point of view in a collective identity.

The problem with "no *I* in *team*" is that, not only is this impossible and untrue in practice, it also forsakes a very valuable tool in building a high-functioning team. Part I of this book asserts that, not only is there an I in team, but also there are as many I's as there are people in the team. And they all must be dealt with before a team can reach its maximum potential.

To better illustrate this, we use the term *singularity* instead of *team*. First, *singularity* does have an *I* (in fact, it has two!), and it helps create a more complex picture of the dynamic of individuality as it relates to collaboration. *Singularity* is a fascinating word in the English language, especially when considering it in the realm of understanding creative collaboration. This is because it provides a dynamic framework for deconstructing the social and cultural forces surrounding most team settings.

SINGULARITY AND INDIVIDUALITY

The first dictionary definition doesn't seem all that complicated: "the state, fact, quality, or condition of being singular."[1] In our many years of observing team environments, the condition of being singular is one of the most obvious yet overlooked and misunderstood phenomena in the practice of collaboration. The misunderstanding derives from the fact that consciousness is, at least at first, an individual enterprise. And this is both the paradox and paramount challenge in transforming our identities from individual to collective when working in collaborative spaces. The problem is that we must simultaneously remember (be acutely aware of) and forget (let go of) our singularity when functioning in collaborative environments.

The basic problem with singularity is that it's very easy to take it for granted and not to consider its effect(s) on others. It may be "normal" to individuals who possess it, but it is definitely not "normal" to those outside it. And we are not immediately conscious of our very specific cultural programing and its effect on our behaviors and views of the world. Most individuals who enter team environments for the first time do not normally have highly developed critical understandings of themselves, their worldviews, and their behaviors, so very often they are discovering such aspects of their identities at the same time as learning how to work with others.

SINGULARITY AND ASTROPHYSICS

The second definition of singularity is much more complex: "a point at which a function takes an infinite value, especially in space-time when matter is infinitely dense, as at the center of a black hole."[2] When scientists are asked about what happened before the Big Bang, they often cite singularity: "Most physicists," explains MIT physicist Alan Lightman, "believe that in this quantum era, the entire observable universe was roughly a million billion billion times smaller than a single atom."[3]

At some point, as the density of this smaller-than-a-single-atom universe approached infinite levels, it could no longer contract, and an explosion of unimaginable force thrust dense and hot neutrons, protons, electrons, anti-electrons, photons, and neutrinos outward in chaos. As the universe continued to expand, these particles cooled and slowly formed attractions to each other, which resulted in the matter that we know today. Out of singularity-driven chaos came the relative order of the universe we live in.

What does all this have to do with collaboration? In short, chaos and transformation. Being an individual and being a team are two completely different directions of being: different rules, different dynamics, and different outcomes. The force of our singularity contracts inward, while the force of collaboration expands outward. The transformation to team being is at first chaotic but ultimately ordered. It is helpful to see collaboration as a stress-inducing transformation, even after one is an experienced collaborator.

Teamwork is by no means a simple process. It is an alternative state of mind and ultimately being, which is at least one reason it is so difficult. We are taught how to be individual human beings from the day we are born—to walk, to dream, and so on. And even though part of that teaching includes how to relate to other humans, we are surprisingly ill prepared to work well with others in teams *as individual human beings*. This is because many of the fundamental forces of individuality are directed inwardly toward individual benefit rather than outwardly toward collective benefit. Just wanting to work with others is not enough to affect the complex transformation necessary to collaborate. It takes time, patience, discipline, and sometimes pain.

What does it mean to be an individual versus a team? It comes down to where we locate ourselves: inside or outside. It sounds easy, but it's not. Transforming our being from inside (singularity) to outside (collaborative) is not like throwing a switch. It is more like a crisis that feels like chaos.

SINGULARITY AND INITIAL CONDITIONS

It is useful to think of creative collaboration as a form of chaos. This is partly because chaos is an often-mentioned description of what real-life collaboration feels like in the beginning. Like chaos, collaboration may seem at first unpredictable, perhaps even random, but eventually patterns of order materialize. Chaos theory is very helpful in making sense of complex forces operating around collaboration. One of the first steps in applying a chaos-theory lens to a complex phenomenon is to identify initial conditions. This is because patterns and behaviors in chaotic realms are extremely sensitive to initial conditions.

In teamwork, the single most influential initial condition we have observed with hundreds of nascent creative teams is *the individual*. Think of individuals as data points in a collaborative setting. The concept of "sensitivity to initial conditions" applied to individuals in team settings would say that collaboration dynamics are highly sensitive to individual conditions by nature. This makes sense in a very basic way, but in fact, it is something that is often ignored in the practice of creative collaboration. The simple fact is that we cannot separate individuals and the dynamics that surround them from the collaborative process.

The everyday practice of creative collaboration can eventually grow away from the limits imposed by initial conditions (individual members) but not unless they are first recognized, accepted, and confronted. This is why we begin our examination of creative collaboration with a focus on the unpredictable undercurrents of each individual being who enters a collaborative space.

Before we can effectively function "outside the box" of our respective singularities, it is essential that we take time to recognize, accept, and understand what is "inside the box" of our singular mind-sets—both conscious and unconscious—that we bring into collaborative experiences.

Chapter One

A Hero's Quandary

In her recent column on the future of work in a looming age of artificial intelligence, London Business School professor and Future of Work Consortium founder Lynda Gratton draws an interesting parallel between the early years of the Industrial Revolution and the state of affairs in the current day. She sees similarities in the abounding confusion created by new technologies and the ways it can undermine and ultimately redefine the nature of everyday work. "This period, termed Engels' Pause in Britain," she writes, "resulted in deep unhappiness and a reduction in productivity before people upskilled and society was redesigned."[1]

Named after German philosopher Friedrich Engels, Engels' Pause was a documented downturn in the early nineteenth-century livelihood of British workers in response to an era of exponential change.[2] As technology and innovation of the Industrial Age essentially vaporized the need for existing worker skills, worker wages fell, owner profits rose, and a generation of workers was economically paralyzed. The Industrial Age demanded skills the workforce at the time did not have nor ever would have. This resulted in a systemic pause, while a new generation of workers slowly adapted to meet the demands of an entirely different kind of work.

THE RISING STOCK OF SOFT SKILLS

Gratton's warning to the current exponential change in technology and the work around it is that we face a very similar "Engels' Pause," a catch-22 threat. As hard skills—currently well covered in the spectrum of education and worker preparation—become increasingly mechanized, there is a rising premium on soft skills, like empathy, context sensing, collaboration, and creative thinking. These are skills that machines have not yet mastered, and there is an urgency to quickly adapt skill sets for the jobs of the near future. The only problem is, these increasingly valued skill sets are not as easy to find in current systems of education as traditional hard skills.

Soft skills, such as working well with others, don't fit neatly into the monomythic underpinnings of higher education. The college experience is in many ways structured as a hero's journey. An individual (hero) receives a call to action (acceptance letter), and then, in the words of Joseph Campbell, "ventures forth from the world of common day [home] into a region of supernatural wonder [college campus]: fabulous forces are there encountered [learning] and a decisive victory is won [degree]: the hero comes back from this mysterious adventure with the power to bestow boons on his fellow man [huge ego]."[3]

Enter, the *hero's quandary*. Students educated to take over the world with their fresh diplomas enter a workforce, where the soft skills they've brushed aside or simply not practiced are now at a premium. Learning these skills on the job becomes trial by fire. In the creative media classes where we work, it usually begins with something like, "I intend to be the next [insert name of great filmmaker or showrunner, studio boss, successful entrepreneur or influencer]." The idea of creator as *auteur* is romantic notion that has been ingrained in public consciousness from the beginning of the storytelling industries: to become a creator whose personal influence and artistic control are so great, their very identity is as important as (or perhaps more important than) the story itself.

Despite slow advances in recent years, it remains surprisingly difficult to extract from young minds the fallacy that their future work life is a singular enterprise. Part of the challenge comes from the fact that current leaders in the creative fields were educated and indoctrinated in a time when a hero's-journey approach to the field was simply the way things were done. This could be why, at least until very recently, the creative industries have had notoriously terrible reputations when it comes to the practice of working well with others.

The problem with a hero's approach to just about any major field—from education to engineering to media to medicine—is that in actual practice they are now social enterprises. The hero needs to go on a new journey. The hero needs to learn how to work well with others. And the auteur is dead.

For some time now, we have witnessed a paradigmatic pause of sorts when it comes to preparing dream seekers in training (filmmakers, TV producers, screenwriters, entrepreneurs) for success in their creative industries. It is increasingly out of fashion to be calling yourself a lone genius (auteur). This is because, according to professionals who are hiring now, the most sought-after attribute in the new workforce, no matter how brilliant the candidate may be, is the ability to work well with others.

Professionals in all sectors of the media industry tell us over and over, "If you can just teach them how to work well with others (and of course how to form an intelligent sentence or two in writing), we can pretty much handle the rest." And this emerging paradigm shift in the importance of collaborative skills is clearly not unique to the creative storytelling cohort we focused on in our research. It is systemic across most fields.

For example, the World Economic Forum, an international not-for-profit foundation focused on engaging the foremost political, business, and other leaders of society to shape global, regional, and industry agendas see the era of work we are entering as the "fourth industrial revolution." In *The Future of Jobs*, they conclude,

> On average, by 2020, more than a third of the desired core skill sets of most occupations will be comprised of skills that are not yet considered crucial to the job today, according to our respondents.
>
> Overall, social skills—such as persuasion, emotional intelligence and teaching others—will be in higher demand across industries than narrow technical skills, such as programming or equipment operation and control. In essence, technical skills will need to be supplemented with strong social and collaboration skills.[4]

Similarly, in 2012, IBM commissioned a study involving more than 1,700 CEOs and senior public-sector leaders from around the globe to identify similar trends and challenges ahead for the worlds of work. They found, "CEOs have a new strategy in the unending war for talent. They are creating more open and collaborative cultures—encouraging employees to connect, learn from each other and thrive in a world of rapid change. Collaboration is the number one trait CEOs are seeking in their employees, with 75 percent of CEOs calling it critical."[5]

Multinational professional services network Deloitte charts the stunning rise in social enterprise across the globe. Deloitte's 2016 *Global Human Capital Trends* study identifies significant implications for future workers:

Among the 7,000+ companies who responded (in over 130 countries), the #1 issue on leaders' minds is "how to redesign our organizational structure" to meet the demands of the workforce and business climate today.

The conclusion, after almost a year of study, is that today's digital world of work has *shaken the foundation* of organizational structure, shifting from the traditional functional hierarchy to one Deloitte calls a *"network of teams."* This new model of work is forcing us to change job roles and job descriptions; rethink careers and internal mobility; emphasize skills and learning as keys to performance; redesign how we set goals and reward people; and change the role of leaders.[6]

Deloitte's *2018 Global Human Capital Trends* report extends the impact of a drastically shifting work paradigm beyond the workforce to the bottom line:

> Based on this year's global survey of more than 11,000 business and HR leaders, . . . organizations are no longer assessed based only on traditional metrics such as financial performance, or even the quality of their products or services. Rather, organizations today are increasingly judged on the basis of their relationships with their workers, their customers, and their communities, as well as their impact on society at large—transforming them from *business* enterprises into *social* enterprises.
>
> . . . Building these relationships challenges business leaders to listen close-ly to constituents, act transparently with information, break down silos to enhance collaboration, and build trust, credibility, and consistency through their actions. This is not a matter of altruism: Doing so is critical to maintain-ing an organization's reputation; to attracting, retaining, and engaging critical workers; and to cultivating loyalty among customers.[7]

When it comes to the practice of collaboration, the writing is clearly on the wall. The skill of working well with others is at a premium when it comes to being relevant in emerging work paths. Increasingly, employers are saying, "We don't need superheroes. We need people who know how to work well with other people."

WHAT IS A HERO TO DO?

This hero's quandary (a vulnerability exposed in response to an unexpected or unnatural challenge) is actually a necessary first step in transitioning to any team environment—regardless if an individual is skilled in working well with others. Team being is a state of mind that must be called on in a conscious way.

In Western culture, children are raised from birth to be individuals. Attention and nurturing come from an outside world in the form of parental figures and are imparted on individual identities. When children reach school age, they are educated to be productive individuals.

Learning and progress through education is similarly received from outside in: Learning is distributed from "knowing" educational figures toward the growth, betterment, and preparation of students to independently enter "real worlds" beyond education. This is why it is entirely natural for individuals to pause when entering collaborative environments, where the direction of attention shifts from individual interests to collective interests. Individuals have largely underdeveloped social compasses to maneuver in collective environments. In an individualistic culture, independence and assertiveness are scope values, whereas in a collective culture, the scope values are relational in terms of being attentive to the needs of others, helpful to others, dependable with others, and generous to others.

Under collectivism the focus is on the group rather than the individual. In the individualistic culture the focus is on being independent rather than identifying with a group. American culture has been primarily individualistic, with current forces attempting to push it more to a collectivistic culture. The hero's quandary—essentially cooperating with others before "saving the world with individual brilliance"—is a first cue that a shift in one's individual state of mind is required.

THE CHALLENGE OF TEAMWORK

The most sensible way forward for heroes in waiting is to hang up the cape and learn how to work well with others on the job. Even though upbringing and educational systems in Western culture are individual centered, it likely that individuals have had some sorts of team experiences throughout life. For instance, family is a form of collaboration and collective undertaking. In addition, most sports practices are built on the idea of team: all for one and one for all. Also, many forms of music, dance, and arts require careful collaboration. And just about everyone has worked on some sort of group project in school. Though raised to be highly individual, we still have exposure to various forms of teamwork.

The problem with these types of team experiences is that they are very inconsistent. They do not usually get beyond the thin surface of team practices, and more often than not, they lead to a slight distaste for the practice of teamwork. When we talk to new group members about their previous experiences in working in teams, we expect to get a fair amount of rolled eyes, sighs, and shaking heads—on the whole, not good. They consistently cite unexpectedly common experiences in typical team settings: the self-appointed leader (dictators); the free riders (lazy ones hiding from work); and the overarching feeling of "I could have done this better by myself." Other problems they often describe:

• One or a very few in a team end up doing all the work.
• Someone inevitably hijacks the role as group leader, and it's usually the person who is least qualified to lead.
• There is a great amount of destructive infighting.
• Participants can count on "being stuck with the bad ones" in their team.
• Though not always a terrible experience, teamwork more often than not is a negative experience.

As collaboration is increasingly recognized as vital element of the twenty-first-century workplace, even the academy has shown increasing interest in the phenomenon. At least a few times each year, our faculty is called to large meetings, where the room is arbitrarily broken into smaller groups for follow-up discussions. For us, these team settings generate the same feelings on past teamwork experiences we and our students have had: not good.

Working creatively and constructively together in a creative collaborative project team does not occur naturally. Just labeling a collection of ten or twenty people a "team" is, in itself, not enough to have a creative, high-performing team. And this is unfortunately how most teams experience are initiated—in essence, "Go be a team."

There are some basic problems with this *collaborate-on-the-fly* approach:

• Teamwork is *not* common sense and is therefore prone to missteps fueled by individual instinct, especially by team leaders. The foundations of Western society are built on hierarchical, authoritarian systems of performance, from parent to teacher; most work settings are built on the fundamental focus on pleasing one's boss. This is a crucial detriment to effective collaboration.
• Team leaders are more often than not ill equipped to effectively impart team skills on the job. There is an assumption that everyone in the room knows how to be a team, but they do not and therefore operate more often in unconscious heroic opposition with each other than in collaboration.

Dealing with these individual "elephants in the room" requires patience, guidance, nurturing, and time, none of which most work environments have in surplus.

- The practice of collaboration is fraught with paradoxes that require understanding and courage to apply. In many situations of collaboration, there are contradictions in place that require high levels of critical assessment—for instance, the simultaneous need for dictatorship and democracy or the preaching against overattentiveness to "authority" by an authority—be it a teacher, author, or boss.

If a thrown-together collection of people looks for a model of "best practices" in everyday team environments, they will more likely find dysfunctional tactics than best practices. Using the word *team* as if it had a specific, clear meaning is a form of word magic implying that the collection of people so labeled assign the same meaning to the work and have the skills necessary to work creatively and constructively with each other.

Teamwork is an entirely distinct state of being apart from individuality. It needs a space for incubation and cultivation—the space that educational environments can provide but work environments, as a rule, cannot. Teamwork takes time to develop and take hold.

Chapter Two

Thinking inside the Box

Imagine yourself—everything you are as a human being—in the form of *a box*. Within that box we can find your history, traits, cultural programming, quirks, dreams, insecurities, beliefs, secrets, and everything that makes you who you are. Now imagine that you, in the form of this box, are placed into a room with other people, also in the form of boxes that represent *their* individual beings (singularities), to perform a task together.

Because we human beings are social creatures by nature, we'll likely find some sort of map in our respective boxes that can guide us as we step into a collaborative experience. This is why working in a team is not an entirely foreign experience. Teamwork is something we're conditioned to think we know how to do.

As we step into a team setting, we are likely to simply step out of the boxes of our individual identities into a team realm, assuming that others in the team possess the same or similar maps. At this point, individuals access their respective maps on how to work with others and begin working together. This is an example of a commonsense approach to team relations by *thinking outside our boxes*. When we enter a team situation, we step out of our boxes to be part of a team outside our protective individual realms and proceed into team relations and outcomes. By stepping outside our boxes, we are choosing to make our boxes invisible.

The problem with these invisible boxes we all bring into team environments is that they are still in the room. So, we trip over them all of the time as we try to collaborate. However selfless or altruistic that thinking outside the boxes of our individual mind-sets may seem for teamwork, it is equally important that we critically assess what is inside our boxes and the boxes of other team members before we can maximize our effectiveness in working together.

THE PARADOX OF PERSONAL AND SOCIAL IDENTITY

Media scholar David Buckingham aptly illustrates how complex the idea of thinking inside and outside the boxes of our personal and social identities can be:

> The fundamental paradox of identity is inherent in the term itself. From the Latin root *idem*, meaning "the same," the term nevertheless implies both similarity and difference. On the one hand, identity is something unique to each of us that we assume is more or less consistent (and hence the same) over time. . . . Yet on the other hand, identity also implies a relationship with a broader collective or social group of some kind. When we talk about national identity, cultural identity, or gender identity, for example, we imply that our identity is partly a matter of what we share with other people. Here, identity is about identification with others whom we assume are similar to us (if not exactly the same), at least in some significant ways. [1]

Critically considering what we bring into collaborative spaces as individuals is necessary in teamwork but clearly a complex and difficult process. Like so many other dynamics involved in collaboration, it is not a simple switch to flip. The following example illustrates this complexity in action.

BEING THE BOSS

Danielle was ecstatic when her team agreed by consensus to make her their group leader. This was something that she had always dreamed of, and the fact that her peers saw her as the right person for this role was particularly meaningful to her.

One of her first challenges involved casting actors for the lead role. The deadline for casting decisions had passed. A small group of her peers who were overseeing casting asked for more time, which put Danielle in the ultimate position of being a leader: having to make difficult decisions. If more time was taken to find the right person, then the production schedule would be compromised, and there would be added stress in getting the project finished. The casting group argued that finding the right person to be the lead actor was worth the risk of getting behind schedule. To Danielle, a self-defined rational, organized, and deliberate decision maker, this was a no-brainer: A deadline is a deadline. They would go with the best actor they had, and production would go forward as scheduled.

Danielle was surprised when the casting team pushed back forcefully on her decision. They felt that the series the team was making was good and deserved the best possible effort in casting the right actors for roles, even if that meant putting the team a little behind schedule. They'd rather face the challenge of catching up with the schedule than compromising the quality of acting. Conflicts like this bring out both the best and worst in team practices, and this one revealed a very important distinction between individual perspectives and collective perspectives.

When Danielle's decision was questioned by her teammates, her first, beautifully honest reaction was, "I just don't understand. I am the boss, and it's my turn to say no." Danielle's preconceived, singular perception of being a leader was the right to say no, like leaders in her past collaborative experiences had modeled for her. However right Danielle's decision might have been for the team did not matter in the context of her individually held expectations of how leaders in her past had operated and in turn taught her how to operate when she was in a position of leadership. Danielle's decision was clear and correct within her individuality; it was a very different matter for others outside her individual realm.

"Boxes" of individual perceptions are conscious and unconscious aspects of individual identity and experience that every team member brings into a collaborative setting. At some point in the collective experience, they must be brought into view, identified, understood, and dealt with. The sooner this is done in the collaborative process, the more time there is to effectively face challenges down the road of collaboration.

PHYSICS OF SINGULARITY

At the beginning of a team, each member enters as a singular individual, most likely with a singularity mind-set, where they are concerned predominantly with what they know and value. It is helpful to think of a singular mind-set like a nucleus of a cell and a team project as an opportunity to create fusion with other nuclei. Fusion is the process of combining two or more distinct entities into a new whole. It has been the focus of scientific curiosity for some time now as an alternative and sustainable energy source with minimal byproducts. Nuclear fusion, like teamwork, is very difficult to accomplish. This is because nuclei have a built-in force of repulsion—Coulomb Force—that discourages fusion.[2] This is very similar to the dynamic around individuals in social settings: There is a natural resistance to open up our individuality to peers in a social realm.

Over time, scientists have discovered techniques to make fusion more possible and their techniques are conceptually helpful in considering the challenge of singular mind-sets in collaborative settings. The first technique is to minimize repulsive forces: Find lighter elements with fewer and weaker repelling forces (isotopes of hydrogen fused with helium). In team settings, think of this strategy as building self-awareness of natural forces of repulsion due to individual incompatibility and indifference. If we can work to identify factors of individuality that get in the way of collective interests, then we can increase the chances of effective collaboration.

The second is acceleration. When the nuclear particles are accelerated, their levels of attraction increase and lead to fusion. In team settings, this can be accomplished by working with each other over time. Action is a necessary element for building effective collaboration. We cannot simply will effective collaboration into existence. It needs some form of energy and action to take hold.

Fusion is the goal in collaboration. But the road to it is complicated by the depth of individual identities, especially the out-of-awareness aspects of their singularity.

EXPLORING THE SINGULAR MIND-SET

In their singularity, individual team members each carry an "inside-the-box" mind-set formed by their cultural programing, psychohistories, and conditioned responses to authority. The singular mind-set is a vital force that affects the way the team develops. Such mindsets need to be understood to move to a collective connected mind-set that ultimately materializes in a well-functioning team.

If you watch team members' behaviors closely during the initial period of team formation, you will likely see through their body language, anxiety and apprehension. You might see someone attempt to grab control of the group as members struggle with issues of inclusion, control, and openness. The control issue centers around who defines the process and direction the group takes. More specifically it determines what the team spends its time doing.

You may notice that the team members attempt to act as if they have no anxiety or apprehensions, but their body language speaks volumes. They act as if they cannot openly discuss what they are really feeling and thinking at the moment of entry.

Yet, in reality, they are free to relate any way they want; they are only limited by their seemingly invisible cultural programing, psychohistory, and imagination. They have likely never been explicitly told that they cannot openly discuss their emotions and feelings as the team unfolds or, for that matter, the nonverbal body language enacted by the team.

Rules (real, imagined, or resulting from cultural programming or unconscious psychohistory messages) are like an "inside-the-box" that channels behavior and focus for members of a creative team. It is probably not coincidental that the popular phrase "think outside the box" is often evoked during discussions about creativity. Actually getting outside the box is not easy, especially due to the lack of awareness of what is inside the box that each team member brings to the team.

Within our inside-the-box cultural programing, there are many largely implicit "rules" that are acquired outside of immediate awareness, so they have not been subjected to conscious reasoning and choice. Cultural programming consists of the norms a culture inculcates about appropriate behavior in relationships, mostly vicariously, through observation and copying behavior.

In a sense, they are basically invisible to team members' conscious awareness. As team members enter the team, their "inside-the-box" is activated. They tend to operate in the realm of the unconscious and early social and interpersonal learning through mirror neurons and cultural programing. Team members do not perceive the world with pristine eyes but from the "inside-the-box" perspective they carry into the team.

As previously mentioned, at the inception of a team, it is easy to notice that individuals do not openly express their emotions or honest personal perspective about what is actually taking place between members of the team. It is fairly well established that we learn to relate to others from our early caretakers. There is even some research that suggests much of this early learning is injected into us by mirror neurons before we learn language. Mirror neurons are a type of brain cell that responds equally either when someone performs an action or when they observe someone else perform the same action.[3]

Some researchers studying mirror neurons believe that these neurons help explain how and why we seem to be able to grasp the emotions of others and feel empathy for them. If watching an action and performing that action can activate the same parts of the brain, then it may make sense that observing a behavior and performing a behavior could also elicit the same feelings in people. The concept might appear simple, but its implications are far-reaching. For example, recent studies in neurobiology indicate the experiences with our early caretakers shape our neural circuitry between twelve and eighteen months of age, and it happens entirely in our implicit memory outside our awareness.[4]

Early relational development can sometimes significantly influence collaborative team dynamics negatively and destructively.[5] While it is not possible to redo our past behavior, we are managed by it to the extent that we are unaware of how it influences us in the present. The interpersonal pattern from our early caretakers becomes the template for interpersonal relations throughout our lives. Our brains, however, have neural plasticity, which means they have an innate capacity to generate new neurons throughout our lives.[6] We are capable of creating new neural circuitry that permits us to relate in new, creative, and more resilient ways. And most importantly, we can store those new ways of relating in our conscious awareness while learning about our unconscious, limited, and perhaps dysfunctional ways of relating.

From the standpoint of psychohistory, there are also relationship messages that can be injected into us unconsciously that influence how we relate to team members. Such relational messages as "Big boys (or girls) don't cry," "There is nothing to be afraid of," "Suffer in silence," "Don't talk back," "Color inside the lines" and "You really have no imagination" can become deeply embedded and operate as invisible rules for relating to other team members. These messages become an "invisible box" each of us carries when we enter a team.

We have found that few people have been explicitly taught how to label and constructively express the feelings they have about themselves and their relationships to others while working together. For example, it is clear that, for a collaborative creative team to excel, team members need to be unguardedly open about their thoughts and feelings, both negative and positive, during the collaborative process. Though it may sound easy, it really isn't. Despite the fact that all team members are always experiencing and having thoughts and feelings, there are a plethora of hidden factors that stymie open expression within the team. We uncover this mystery in the coming pages.

Every member of a team also walks in with conscious and unconscious learning about the role of authority in organizations, which they most likely vicariously learned through cultural programing and their psychohistory with their early caretakers. Through cultural programming, team members are often imbued with the existential script message of (1) doing whatever someone in authority wants, even though they disagree or have reservations about it, and (2) doing it without openly complaining or openly expressing salient emotions. They all hope for a favorable evaluation by the authority figure.

Children learn that it is socially unacceptable to openly disagree and express their reservations or lack of understanding of what an authority figure is requesting. They learn to silently sit and pay attention, perhaps daydreaming to cope with the deadened feelings. They look to authority figures to tell them what is meaningful in their work lives without much conscious thought and reflection. They learn to compete with their peers and focus on an authority figure's definition of what is really important for them to do. It is the authority figure's vision of what is worth knowing and talking about.

Having never been explicitly taught collaboration skills, it is not surprising that most team members carry the orientation and mental map they learned in their early school experiences into the organization or team, where they become preoccupied with pleasing their authority figure or avoiding criticism from them. They learn to put on a "game face" and try to become skilled at anticipating what an authority figure wants while being reluctant to challenge or criticize them for fear of falling from their good graces. They mistakenly believe that there is nothing they can learn from their peers. Because they are not taught how to collaborate, especially creatively, it is not at all surprising that they show up in organizations without the necessary skills for creative collaboration.

Milgram's studies on obedience to authority, as well as studies on such cult groups as Jim Jones's People's Temple or Heaven's Gate, attest to the primitive, unreflective, and unconscious compliance with an authority figure's definition of what aspects of reality are to be given attention.[7] More importantly, team members have yet to develop a collective, connected mind-set. They are still very much caught up in an individual mind-set.

Culturally, asking about or reflecting on what other team members may be feeling in team settings is taboo. This is the way in which psychohistory and cultural programing can significantly influence collaborative team dynamics in a negative, destructive way. That is unnecessary, as we hope to demonstrate in our deeper analysis of creative team dynamics.

In terms of cultural programing, we have consistently found that most team members' initial experiences of teamwork have been individually driven and competitive in nature. They have not had exposure to or experience in developing the constructive teamwork skills necessary for creative collaboration. When asked directly how they learned to work in a team, team members never mention someone actually teaching them the requisite skills. More often than not, they are simply accustomed to working independently and somewhat competitively while focusing on figuring out what an authority figure wants.

We have found from our experience that openly talking about individual perspectives of team members—be they good, bad, or ugly—helps bring it into their awareness in such a way that they experiment with doing something different to get "outside the boxes" of their individuality. They become more aware of ways they have unnecessarily limited themselves in creative collaboration with other members of a creative team.

Our intent is to bring into awareness common social conditioning in order to effectively confront dysfunctional, wired-in team behavior.[8] You will discover what is inside the box you are bringing into a team. Hopefully, with increased awareness of the invisible and unconscious forces, you will come away with a new mental map of what it takes for you and other members of your team to perform at the highest possible level in collectively creating something out of nothing. You will, of course, have to actually engage in personally developing the skills and applying them within a creative team.

EXERCISING SELF-AWARENESS IN COLLABORATIVE SETTINGS

There is a widely used group exercise called the Social Identity Wheel that we have found effective in sensitizing individuals to better understand and practice the art of *thinking inside the box*.[9] We discovered this exercise in an inclusive teaching workshop designed for college teachers. The exercise helps to illuminate the incredibly complex yet often-unacknowledged elements of identity in every classroom.

The exercise begins with a personal reflection of yourself through different lenses of identity. These are lenses that we often don't think about, don't share, or assume others know implicitly about us:

Race	Ethnicity
Gender	Sex
Religious or spiritual affiliation	National origin
Age	First language
(Dis)ability	Socioeconomic status
Sexual orientation	

The reflection centers on considering how you process your own identity along the lines of these lenses:

- The aspects of your identity you think about most often and least often
- The aspects of your identity that you would like to learn more about
- Which identities have the strongest effect on how you perceive yourself
- Which identities have the strongest effect on how others perceive you

Like other forces surrounding teamwork, self-awareness is not a switch to flip on. It is a process that takes time. The first step is to become more conscious of the individual identities we bring into social and collaborative settings. Exercising individual awareness of what we each bring into social spaces is a helpful thought process to build a constructive social awareness, in essence being conscious of how we are perceived by others. If we cannot effectively transform our singular mind-sets into collective mind-sets, then we are likely to fall short of maximizing synergies between individuals, and we are prone to dysfunctional team practices that only benefit one or a few members of the team.

Ultimately, we are doing our collaborative partners a favor by thinking inside the box of the singular mind-sets we bring into team environments before rushing into the world of a team outside those mind-sets. When we think inside the box of our identities, we can begin to recognize, accept, and effectively adapt our singular frames of mind to meet team objectives. The better we can see each other's boxes in the room of our collaboration, the more likely we are to build empathy for each other, which is vital to effectively work together.

Part II

Vulnerability

"We love seeing raw truth and openness in other people, but we're afraid to let them see it in us. We're afraid that our truth isn't enough—that what we have to offer isn't enough without the bells and whistles, without editing and impressing."—Brené Brown[1]

In many ways, the male bird of paradise is a poster child for the concept of vulnerability as it relates to effective teamwork. This fascinating creature located deep in the forests of New Guinea's West Papua Province is notorious for its dazzling mating rituals that involve remarkably bizarre movements, sounds, and visual displays of color and variety. "Here in New Guinea it isn't nature tooth and claw, but nature with painted skirt and crowned brow—a bird drag show," says evolutionary biologist Ed Scholes.[2] It is difficult to watch these outlandish mating dances without asking, "Why do they perform these bizarre rituals of denying what they really are? You're an insecure bird!"

If you watch a creative team when they first get together, you are likely to see a bird-of-paradise-like move or two from team members as the team begins to take shape. Instead of shapeshifting with feathers, team members use posture, voice, and gesture to mask what they truly are (scared, nervous, weak) with a colorful variety of illusions, like strength, indifference, confidence, pleasantness, and unblinking acceptance of whatever comes their way.

Instead of loud calls and stylized dancing, group members do such things as quickly moving to people in the group who look and act like them, assuming leadership without invitation, building facades of harmony, and focusing attention on authority figures. It is difficult to watch these stunning deceptions without asking, "Why do they perform these bizarre rituals of denying what they really are? You're a terrified and vulnerable human being!"

The thing is, there is a reason for the real birds of paradise to act like they do. Ed Scholes pins it down to basic biology:

> It may look whacky, it may look funny. But these behaviors didn't evolve to be whacky and funny.
>
> They evolved through sexual selection by female choice to be precise, choreographed things that these males do time and time again, day after day, throughout their whole lives specifically to be attractive to females during courtship.
>
> The male mating dances help the female bird decide which male traits and behaviors will pass down to the next generation. In New Guinea an abundance of food and a scarcity of predators have allowed the birds to flourish and to exaggerate their most attractive traits to a degree that even literal-minded scientists have called absurd. [3]

But there is no sensible explanation for the "dances around vulnerability" that teams engage in when they first get together. This is why one of the first challenges that members of a creative team confront is the instinctually artful aversion of vulnerability. Vulnerability is a force most people tend to run away from and avoid.

The challenge here is in reframing vulnerability as a positive and healthy state of mind. It is the foundation for constructively building on the emotional undercurrent of fear, failure, risk, conflict, differences, and authority. In order for there to be vulnerability in the creative team, the team members need to accept and embrace with courage all the underlying emotional undercurrents.

Vulnerability basically is an emotionally tinged state that we experience when we confront uncertainty, emotional and intellectual exposure, and risky decisions. As Brené Brown suggests, it is about having the courage to do something even when the outcome of an action cannot be predicted. [4] In order to be vulnerable, we need to accept and embrace our perceived weaknesses so they don't simmer in a destructive manner.

Clearly, all of this has to do with team members confronting their fears of being vulnerable and learning how to support and co-mentor each other.

There is often a belief that being vulnerable by expressing emotions, feelings, and different perspectives is not important in collaboration and is perhaps dangerous. This is reflected by such injunctions as "Leave your feelings at the door" or the more pejorative "Let's avoid touchy-feely stuff" or even "Don't take it personally" and "If you can't say something nice, don't say anything." The norms against vulnerability—in not expressing feelings and emotions in work relationships—are deeply ingrained in our culture.

The reality is that we all in fact have emotions and perspectives about what we are involved in when we are in collaboration together. Many of us have learned how to suppress them and pretend they don't exist. We learn to put on a game face to mask our true emotions and perspectives about what is taking place in the team as it evolves.

Most of us live in a culture that discourages introspection and emotional openness in relationships, particularly in the context of work. We are accustomed to engaging in social rituals, roles, and pretense in each other's presence rather than expressing our actual experiences with each other as we work together more openly and deeply.

Cultural conditioning outside of our awareness results in much pretense in our relationships, which function as social walls that keep us from knowing either ourselves or another at a deep emotional level. We vicariously learn not to express our actual emotional inner experience about what we see and feel taking place among our team members. We mostly implicitly learn not to be open and vulnerable with others. We are in many ways an emotion-phobic culture. Few of us have been explicitly taught to identify our basic emotions and how to express them constructively in our work relationships. This is changing somewhat because some elementary schools are teaching children how to identify and express their emotions constructively when working with others. But the most important thing for a creative team to learn is how to constructively connect with the emotional currents that promote creativity as a collective act.

SHARED VULNERABILITY

In his book *The Culture Code*, Daniel Coyle points out what is likely the most important aspect of vulnerability in the context of creative collaboration: seeing vulnerability as a social, shared act rather than an exclusively personal liability. This involves, he writes, "the willingness to perform a certain behavior that goes against our every instinct: sharing vulnerability."[5]

The chapters in part II dig deeply into the ground of everyday vulnerabilities: uncertainty, fear, failure, authority, and difference. Exploring these vulnerabilities is not undertaken to reveal weakness; rather, it is to identify opportunities to build collaborative strength.

Coyle uses the term *vulnerability loops*, or shared exchanges of openness, as the most basic building block of cooperation and trust in successful teams. He explains,

> Vulnerability loops seem swift and spontaneous from a distance, but when you look closely, they all follow the same discrete steps:
>
> 1. Person A sends a signal of vulnerability.
> 2. Person B detects this signal.
> 3. Person B responds by signaling their own vulnerability.
> 4. Person A detects this signal.
> 5. A norm is established; closeness and trust increase.

It is the creation of constructive norms around vulnerability that allows us to harness the incredible power of vulnerability in creative collaboration.

Chapter Three

Uncertainty

"The things we fear most in organizations—fluctuations, disturbances, imbalances—are the primary sources of creativity."—Margaret Wheatly [1]

In storytelling terms, we would call it the "inciting action"—a confusing, chaotic, and often-dangerous action, usually directed at the protagonist, that sets the story in motion. With collaborators, the inciting action is the moment their safe sense of self is thrust into an uncontrollable team setting.

We refer to this grave sense of uncertainty as the "big bang" of creative collaboration: the moment a team member enters a creative team environment and they struggle with their individual comfort level and control mechanisms. Like the Big Bang, uncertainty is an ever-expanding force in constant movement away from the comparative certainty of singularity.

Uncertainty is a necessary phase of collaboration and likely the most important phase of effective transformation into a collaborative state of being. The ultimate challenge posed in this first phase of working together is to clearly see and critically examine apparent threats created by confusion, chaos, and complexity as opportunities for growth and strength.

When it comes right down to it, teamwork is scary. This is because there is so little control over it, especially as it compares to the control we have in our singular domains. Not only does it feel scary, chaotic, unpredictable, and unwieldy, but on top of it all, there is absolutely no assurance that a team effort is going to work. "It's like an archaeological dig," writes Ed Catmull, "where you don't know what you're looking for or whether you will even find anything. The process is downright scary." [2] Therefore, we're likely to feel, at some point in the collaboration process, that we are spinning wheels and wasting our time. It not only might fail, but in everyday practice, teams actually can and do fail. Why even bother? Such is the constant presence of uncertainty around teamwork.

Believe it or not, that is OK. In fact, such feelings of uncertainty are a starting point to success. If we can understand, accept and openly discuss this uncertainty, then we can harness its creative energy to instill strength in our creative teams. Embracing uncertainty means being OK with working on a collective objective with no guarantee for success. It requires that team members have the courage to take risk in the face of uncertainty.

THE INHERENT DIFFICULTY OF UNCERTAINTY

The interesting thing about harnessing uncertainty is that, even once you accept it, it is still difficult and against the grain of individual comfort. For instance, while writing this book we were invited by administration to an inclusive teaching methods workshop. The purpose of the meeting was to sensitize faculty to the often-unrecognized learning needs of students.

Like many twenty-first-century large-group gatherings, the meeting included small-group breakout sessions designed to inspire more intimate discussions and ideas. The moment the meeting leaders put us in our respective groups, we felt the surge of vulnerability and uncertainty. Our shared objective was to generate ideas on what we could do better to meet the needs of marginalized learners. The uncertainties surrounding this group effort abounded:

- Is this really necessary?
- Who are these people whom I am supposed to be working with?
- Are they sincere in this group effort? Or do they have the same doubts I do?
- It would be so much easier to do this workshop by myself than having to work with others.
- This is very likely to be a complete waste of time.

Regardless of the group task, whether it is required, desired, unexpected, or something in between, the first step in collaboration brings uncertainty, with no guarantees. Working in a realm of uncertainty requires personal reflection, patience, and persistence, embedded in an overwhelming feeling of doubt. Team members being vulnerable to openly discuss their experience of uncertainty is necessary in moving to a collective mindset.

THE CASE OF RODRIGO'S WALL

"Uncertainty is the ground for imagination and creativity. It is the ground for creating something out of thin air."

Rodrigo had heard these words in class several times already, but he and his teammates in their TV series writers' room were not finding any comfort in them. They had hit a wall in their story and were simply at a loss for ideas. They had come up with a very interesting concept for their story, but the first few versions of their script were not delivering what they had promised. This is a normal part of a collective writing effort: The creative challenge of writing, difficult enough on an individual level, is magnified when multiple writers are working on an idea together.

Creating original content in stories is difficult for a number of reasons. First, it is daunting to come up with an idea that, using filmmaker Michael Rabiger's directing terminology, "cuts across conventional thinking."[3] It is far easier to fall straight in line with conventional thinking and repeat it with empty clichés and stereotypes. This is why film and television battle with the tendency to stick close to proven formulas with sequels, adaptions, and reboots. Originality in storytelling requires first courage—to walk on the high wire of original thinking without a safety net—and then clarity—opening your eyes and mind to the jewels of perspective in your seemingly inconsequential everyday lives.

Upon receiving less-than-enthusiastic notes on his team's third draft, Rodrigo had had enough of the leap-of-faith coaching. He wanted certainty: precise steps leading to precise results. In one grand exclamation of frustration he cried, "But we're just students! How do you expect us to be original? We have limits!"

Rodrigo's honest desperation was a turning point for the group. He had unintentionally identified his team's problem. They had built a wall between what they knew and were certain of and what they were not. They were afraid of coming up with an idea that did not look like other ideas, as if that might reveal their ineptitude as writers. In fact, though, avoiding this uncertainty was freezing their creativity.

Expressing his group's frustration out loud surfaced their vulnerability and allowed for everyone else in the writing team to relate to it and accept it. In addition, it clarified the fact that there was an unnecessary wall in the way of their creativity that they needed to dismantle. It was time to blow through this wall. This group of students was not afraid of creativity, but they were definitely afraid of the uncertainty that surrounded it.

In the simplest of terms, creativity requires change. Creating is bringing something into a world that was not previously in that world, and hopefully for the better. This process of creating something out of nothing takes time and is surrounded by uncertainty. In this sense, creativity and uncertainty are natural partners.

Like other forces involved in collaboration, uncertainty is, on face value, perplexing. In 1927, German physicist Werner Heisenberg developed his Uncertainty Principle to confront similar perplexity in the context of quantum mechanics.[4] The heart of this principle is that everything in the universe behaves like both a particle and a wave at the same time. A particle, like the everyday notion of Rodrigo's TV story, for instance, exists in a single place at any instant in time: We tend to look at elements in our everyday lives as particles with clear, predictable features—a cat or a tree or a story—which bolsters the illusion of certainty in our understanding of the world around us. However, when we define them, certain particles are not at all certain. Particle referencing helps us to make sense of our worlds, but it is an illusion.

Unlike particles, waves—like the *creative evolution* of Rodrigo's TV story—are disturbances spread out in space, like ripples in a pond. Because the wave is spread out and moving, it cannot be reduced to a specific position like a particle can. It is in many different positions at the same time. The best we can do to conceptualize a wave is to consider the momentum of its movement rather than its specific position.

Uncertainty, in this light, is the acceptance of the paradox of our everyday illusion of order and certainty. What this means in the context of creative collaboration is that, if we can loosen the grip of our instincts to seek certainty in creative and collaborative activities, allowing a more dynamic field of play, then we are likely to find a more compatible and less stressful framework to succeed in a creative and collaborative setting.

UNCERTAINTY AND CHAOS

Chaos theory also provides a helpful framework to make sense of and harness uncertainty. The process of the initial forming of a collaborative creative team is often experienced by team members as chaotic; they approach with dread due to the force of uncertainty, which is a very strong undercurrent in creative teams. When we first enter a new team environment, whose reason for being is to collaborative creatively, we confront considerable anxiety and apprehension over many sources of uncertainty. Paradoxically, uncertainty is the ground for creativity itself—it is the chance to create something out of nothing.

It can feel strange and chaotic. Listen to this series of expressions from several members of creative teams:

- "Whenever I enter a new project team, I worry about not being able to make meaningful contributions."
- "I am anxious about whether I will be supported by other group members rather than being shot down by aggressive members."
- "I am concerned about how much influence I can exert over the project and the process we use to put it together."
- "I wonder how open I can be in expressing both my feelings and perspectives in terms of the impressions that other group members form of me."

All of these expressions involve uncertainty. In short, uncertainty feels like "This might not go well." And indeed, this is a possibility, but with systematic and sustained attention, "not going well" becomes unlikely.

Uncertainty is embracing the possibility that we might be wrong. There are no guarantees. This uncertainty in chaos is actually the ground for imagination and creativity—it is the space for experimenting with something and creating something new out of thin air. Indeed, the word *chaos* is an ancient Greek word referring to a primordial void of uncertainty from which everything is created.

In our experience, the evolution to team being is not a clear, linear process but more a seemingly chaotic process determined by shifting valences and mind-sets that team members bring into the teams. There is no real clear path or steps for any team. There is no easy way to escape or reduce the uncertainty.

When the project of a team entails "creativity" as its central focus, it is in actuality an open system that allows for much improvising and unfolding throughout the life of the project. It is an ordered type of chaos that is not predictable in a linear fashion but one that organizes itself around unpredictable team issues that arise as the team evolves. *Chaos* is somewhat of a misnomer because the chaotic system is not caused by totally random events or disorder but rather contains a hidden order within the apparently chaotic disorder.

We use the lens of complexity theory in our approach, which suggests that a complex dynamic phenomenon, such as an ongoing team process, cannot be understood by reducing it to its constituent parts and needs a more holistic approach. In contrast to classical equilibrium-seeking systems theories, complexity theory emphasizes change, imbalance, chaos, and discontinuity in the evolution of the work systems in creative teams.

Complexity theory consists of a set of concepts to explain phenomena surrounding uncertainty that are not explainable by traditional (mechanistic) theories.[5] It integrates ideas derived from such diverse sources as chaos theory, cognitive psychology, computer science, evolutionary biology, general systems theory, fuzzy logic, information theory, and other related fields to cope with natural systems as they actually exist rather than simplifying them by breaking them down into their constituent parts.

All complex systems, such as creative teams, are viewed as networks of many interdependent parts that interact and influence each other. Complexity theory attempts to grasp the dynamics of interconnected, evolving systems. It addresses the inability of mechanistic theories to confront in a constructive manner the stark reality that many everyday phenomena are formidably complex and not easily captured by deterministic, reductionist, linear-type approaches.

Anything that cannot be precisely measured does not exist in this mindset. Subscribing to this mental black box shapes how we look at our world and determines what we focus on and do. It is a form of empirical determinism that views the world as a mechanical system that can be described with precision. It focuses exclusively on what currently exists rather than what might be possible if we were imaginative and experimentally minded to see other ways that we might relate and do things together.

This black-box mind-set is largely invisible and tenacious in its hold on our view and is a helpful metaphor to make sense of creative team dynamics. It is easy to become trapped in this black box, which enables us to avoid the uneasiness of uncertainty. This occurs at a deep, implicit level within us, so that we are rarely aware that we are trapped firmly in a limited mental model.

Albert Einstein captures this well when he states, "Imagination is more important than knowledge. For knowledge is limited, whereas imagination embraces the entire world, stimulating progress, giving birth to evolution."[6] Creative teams are fundamentally open systems, with members coevolving, inventing, and adapting as they collectively unfold their work on a creative project. Complex systems have the capability of creating order out of seeming chaos. It is a nonlinear process among team members during the collaboration of a creative project.[7] High-performing creative teams can bring about diversity in perspectives, knowledge, and expertise, which in turn can lead to more creative outcomes (synergy) than individuals working in a strictly serial manner.[8]

Creative solutions are not just the sum of individual team-member efforts but instead represent genuinely new efforts that emerge from the interaction between the team members. Each team member contributes to a fluid and evolving collective structure through their communicated actions and interactions. This collective structure serves as a dynamic framework for meaning making by team members. Creative ideas are thus attributed to the whole group because their emergence is tied to the collective level arising from their interdependence.[9] This perspective moves away from individual-based explanations of creativity and focuses instead on collective creative moments through collaborative interactions and communication.

RODRIGO'S REWARD

Shortly after Rodrigo's public admission of vulnerability in his creative challenge, others in his writing group became energized. Rodrigo's vulnerability not only helped him, but it also was contagious—inspiring everyone else in the team. They put aside their need for guaranteed success and focused on the creative challenge of accessing their own lives and perspectives for original and authentic elements to support their story. They stopped trying to find instant results and engaged in a more dynamic system of steps toward their goal as vulnerable teammates.

Though their work never got any easier, their persistence and dynamic outlook eventually removed the wall in the way of their creative output. They finished the series and won a national award in recognition for their achievement. The takeaway from this experience is not by any means the award. Many, if not most, creative collaboration achievements go unrecognized publicly. The true reward is the exhilarating feeling of riding the wave of uncertainty together toward an outcome the team is proud of. That was Rodrigo's true reward.

Chapter Four

Fear

". . . nameless, unreasoning, unjustified terror which paralyzes needed efforts to convert retreat into advance."—Franklin D. Roosevelt [1]

Most have likely heard President Roosevelt's famous sentence preceding this statement: "The only thing we have to fear is fear itself." But the sentence that followed it is very helpful for framing the most carnal of vulnerabilities in creative collaboration: fear.

Fear has many faces in day-to-day team relations:

- "I'm afraid of calling out my peers on their disappointing commitment. Who am I to judge them if we are peers?"—Katrina, production manager
- "My biggest fear is failing as cinematographer. Everyone is counting on me, and if I ask for help, that will be a sign of weakness."—Lola, cinematographer
- "I'm afraid that no one else shares my sense of commitment to this project. Why should I put in 110% when others don't put in anything?"—Ellie, producer
- "I'm afraid of rocking the boat. Everyone will be mad if I suggest a better idea. We probably should just get this thing done."—Simon, editor
- "I'm afraid, if we let him direct this scene, he'll make us all look bad."—Harry, directing team
- "I've been in teams like this before. I'm afraid this is going to be a waste of time that I simply do not have."—Isaac, writer

THE FORCE OF FEAR IN TEAMWORK

Fear is a powerful and primitive human emotion meant to aid us in surviving real and imagined dangers. It is also a powerful force at the inception of a creative team, where uncertainty and chaos run at high levels. When we face a perceived threat, our bodies respond in specific ways.

Physical reactions include sweating, metabolic changes, increased heart rate, and high adrenaline levels that make us extremely alert. This physical response is also known as "fight or flight," in which your body prepares itself to either enter combat or run away. This biochemical reaction is likely an evolutionary development. It's an automatic response that is crucial to our survival.

Yet it has also been recognized that both animals and people have other responses to a threat: A person or animal might play dead or just "freeze," yell or scream rather than get physical as a fight response, or isolate as a flight response. As a result, some researchers suggest an expanded version of the fight-or-flight response, namely, "freeze, flight, fight, or fright."[2]

However, there is also a "tend-and-befriend" response to fear; it involves turning to others for help or social support or making a situation less tense, less dangerous, or less uncomfortable in some way.[3] This is more likely to occur when team members are able to be vulnerable and openly express their fears about the creative project to each other.

Being afraid is evidence that someone is at the edge of their comfort zone in confronting the turbulence and uncertainty, even though pushing this edge is where growth and learning occurs. It is where practice transitions to performance—where learning new behavior happens.

Fear is different from terror. Terror pulls us down physically and emotionally. Fear, in contrast, energizes and provides focus for challenge and learning. With uncertainty and anxiety creeping in, we can quickly dismiss challenge and learning and replace fear with its insidious relative: doubt. But how do we transition from fear, doubt, and uncertainty to performance and full engagement?

One of the most challenging parts of uncertainty is a feeling of being out of control. However, being vulnerable and staying open to possibilities allows us to fully engage with the experience. Doing so can provide us with vitality for the experience.

Additionally, we have found in our experience working with creative teams that being able to acknowledge and talk about fears within the team helps refocus the energy, and most team members learn that all the members have fears when entering the team. Moreover, they realize that the courage to take risks is necessary to not be controlled by fear. They learn to feel the fear and not let it stop them from moving forward.

Edwards Deming, the father of lean manufacturing and quality circles, advocates for driving fear out of organization to improve collaboration and performance. He believes that no one can achieve their best performance unless they felt safe and secure.[4] The word *security* comes from the combination of two Latin words: *se*, meaning "without," and *cure*, meaning "fear" or "care." The notions of "without fear," "not afraid to express ideas," and "not afraid to ask questions" all accompany the use of the word *security*.

Fear can take on many faces. A common denominator of fear in any form is impaired performance. The specific types of fear that members of a creative collaborative team have vary and can be manifold. Common fears include fear of failing in personal performance and the performance of the team, fear of conflicts, fear of rejection, fear of being inadequate to contribute meaningfully to the project, and fear of being vulnerable and dealing openly with emotional tensions in the team.

When fear levels in a team are high and team members are afraid to be vulnerable, the creative collaborative process within the team is significantly impaired, as is the possibility of learning from failures. In such instances, team members' energies are defensive rather than collaborative or creative. Creativity is severely restricted and greatly reduced. Perspectives are narrowed. Feelings and emotions become disruptive and disabling. Thinking, problem solving, and action become lethargic, unfocused, or dysfunctional. When fear levels in the team are high enough, the team may become immobilized or destructive. While individuals selected to be members of a creative team are largely free to relate to each other anyway they want, they are limited by the largely hidden underground "invisible box" of cultural programing, their personal psychohistories, and their imaginations.

One can be so terrified of making a mistake and uncomfortable with uncertainty that they avoid taking any risk in their work. It is perfectly normal for team members to experience some level of doubt about success in creative projects. Team members coping with fear of failure will lack confidence in their ideas and abilities. Some experience extreme fear of failure because of the imagined put-downs from others, while others may fear any risk taking. Individuals who fear rejection will hold rigid perfectionistic or unrealistic expectations.

Team members' responses to failure are often linked to traumatic or embarrassing events from their past. Even relatively minor failures in early life experiences surrounded by embarrassment or ridicule can carry over to negative thoughts that prevent them from undertaking new creative challenges.

Without the fear-based bottled-up defensive energy strangling collective creativity, energies of team members are released into creative work together. When it comes to dealing with fear, it is vital that team members need to allow them- selves to be vulnerable and express their fears openly to each other. Doing so actually allows for the development of a supportive network for each team member. One of the most important factors in developing a supportive environment to reduce fear is "psychological safety."[5]

Psychological safety is a shared belief that the team is safe for interpersonal risk taking. It is sometimes defined as being able to express one's self without fear of negative consequences in terms of self-image, job-performance rating, or career development. When the experience of interpersonal safety is minimal, team members tend to fear that admitting ignorance, asking for help, admitting an error, voicing concerns and divergent opinions, or simply being different will have a negative impact on how they are perceived by other team members. Such fears inhibit team learning and development.

The risk of being seen as negative often stops people from delivering honest critical assessments of their teams' performance, which limits the thoroughness and accuracy of collective reflection and collective intelligence. Moreover, people strive to maintain not only their own self-image but also the images of others, a tendency that can inhibit negative feedback. It is well documented that bad news (performance-wise) in corporate circles rarely travels up the power hierarchy, as the fear of being seen as negative has been shown to be more acute in team settings than it might be outside of a team.

Additionally, to avoid disrupting or imposing on others' time and imagined goodwill, team members often do not seek feedback, information, or help. Stated more simply, team members are frequently reluctant to actively seek feedback about their performance from anyone, including other team members who could provide such feedback. Despite the constructive gains that can be obtained from feedback, many team members fail to actively solicit it out of basic fear. Although this can be driven by avoidance of the possibility of hearing something a team member does not want to hear, it also stems from a wish not to be seen as lacking in self-sufficiency or as being too intrusive.

In interpersonally safe environments, team members believe that, if they make errors or fail, then others will not penalize them or think less of them for it. They will, in fact, help them and support them in their improvement efforts. They also believe that others will not resent or penalize them for asking for help, information, or feedback.

When a creative team is grounded in this belief, it fosters the confidence to take risks and thereby gain from the associated benefits of learning from each other and actively seeking feedback from each other. When a team builds a psychologically safe team environment, team members tend to feel accepted and respected and engage in taking risks and also encourage each other to take risks.

A crucial factor in establishing vulnerability and openness is promoting a team culture of interpersonal safety. There is much research on creative teams that supports the importance of an interpersonally safe team culture.[6] An interpersonally safe environment is a place in which team members openly voice ideas, willingly seek feedback, provide honest feedback, engage in energetic collaboration, co-mentor each other, admit fears and mistakes, and deepen their commitment to the collective project. Talking openly about fears of being shot down or failing sets the stage for a more creative working bond between team members. Psychological safety is intended to lower perceived interpersonal risk and encourages risk-taking behavior, such as engagement in learning and out-of-the-box behavior.

As applied to a creative team, *psychological safety* and *interpersonal safety* describe reducing risks related to interpersonal uncertainty. More specially, they describe the perceptions or imagined results of taking interpersonal risks with other team members, where fears of negative consequences from doing so are minimal. Rather there is a sense of confidence among team members that that they will not be intentionally embarrassed, rejected, punished, ridiculed, or disrespected for speaking up with what they are experiencing as they work together, either intellectually or emotionally. For team members to feel comfortable openly expressing different ideas, emotions, questions, or reactions—an essential aspect of team learning and development—a creative team needs to develop and sustain a climate of interpersonal safety for all members.

Psychological or interpersonal safety enables team members to overcome the defensiveness, or learning anxiety, that occurs when they are presented with data that contradict their expectations or hopes. When interpersonal safety is experienced by team members, they more often than not feel free to focus on the collective goals and problem prevention rather than on defensive self-protection or CYA-type behavior.

In its research on one hundred creative teams, Google discovered that one of the vital factors of the highest-performing teams is what they label "psychological safety," which we prefer to label "interpersonal safety" because it is concerned with the relationships among members of a team.[7] It specifically refers to team members feeling safe to take interpersonal risks in being vulnerable and open with each other. Google's People Analytic Unit clearly identifies interpersonal safety as the most important factor in high-performing teams. Google's finding is consistent with other research on the effects of "psychological safety" on a team's creative performance.[8]

Feelings of interpersonal safety directly affect the involvement, engagement, and vitality of team members in doing creative work together. This is clear in one of Google's guides for establishing psychological safety:

1. Team members should not interrupt teammates during conversations because that will establish an interrupting norm.
2. They should demonstrate they are listening by summarizing what people say after they have said it.
3. They should admit what they don't know.
4. They shouldn't end a meeting until all team members have spoken at least once.
5. They should encourage people who are upset to express their frustrations and encourage teammates to respond in nonjudgmental ways.
6. They should call out intergroup conflicts and resolve them through open discussion.[9]

An interpersonally safe team environment promotes divergent thinking, creativity, and risk taking while fostering engagement in exploratory and exploitative learning, thereby facilitating creative team performance. Team members are more likely to offer ideas, admit mistakes, ask for help, or provide feedback if they believe it is interpersonally safe to do so.

Kostopoulos and Bozionelos[10] studied team learning behavior, where task conflict moderated the relationship between (1) interpersonal safety and (2) team learning and team performance. They surveyed more than 600 members of 142 innovation project teams in the information technology and pharmaceutical sectors. Their results indicate that interpersonal safety promoted team learning and creative team performance, an effect that was enhanced by creative abrasion. In sum, an interpersonally safe environment helps to both promote and enable divergent thinking, creativity, risk taking, and energized engagement within creative teams.

Interpersonal safety has been a topic of considerable interest and activity over the past two decades in the fields of management, organizational behavior, social psychology, and health-care management. Evidence from empirical studies conducted in diverse organizational and industrial contexts, across multiple countries and regions (e.g., the United States, Israel, Taiwan), supports the idea that interpersonal safety is a crucial factor in team creativity and effectiveness. Overall, review of the research on interpersonal safety provides important insights about performance in creative teams.

This relationship between interpersonal safety and effective performance is especially important when there is uncertainty and a need for creativity to accomplish the project. In addition, interpersonal safety is particularly relevant for understanding team learning and evolution. Much learning in creative teams takes place in the interpersonal interactions between highly interdependent members, and team learning behaviors can be limited by individual concerns about interpersonal risks or consequences, including learning anxiety created by fears and feelings of incompetence that occur during learning.

Overall, research provides considerable support for the idea that a climate of interpersonal safety can mitigate the interpersonal risks inherent in learning. Creative team members are more likely to offer ideas, admit mistakes, ask for help, or provide feedback if they believe it is safe to do so.

Studies clearly show that team members who experience greater interpersonal safety are more likely to speak up within the team. By speaking up, team members can help challenge the status quo, identify problems or opportunities for improvement, and offer ideas to improve their teams' well-being. Yet, extensive research has shown that speaking up in situations without psychological safety is more often than not experienced as risky.[11] The research on interpersonal safety suggests that mitigating this risk is possible.

Most research has found statistically significant variance in interpersonal safety between teams within organizations; that is, team members working closely together tend to have similar perceptions of interpersonal safety, which vary across teams within the same organization.[12] This body of research offers additional support for the idea that interpersonal safety is a vital component of creative teams.

Much of the literature on interpersonal safety provides relatively little insight regarding how interpersonal safety is established and unfolds, much less on what builds, lessens, or destroys. Interpersonal safety takes time to build through experience and positive responses to displays of vulnerability and other risky actions. It is not clear if it can be destroyed instantly through a negative response. Researchers might well examine the emergent dynamics of interpersonal safety within creative teams in future investigations.

Working collaboratively is an integral part of creative team life but often proves more interpersonally difficult than anticipated. One of the most fundamental challenges creative teams face is how to manage the interpersonal threats inherent in team members admitting ignorance or uncertainty, voicing concerns and opinions, or simply being different. These threats are subtle but powerful, and they inhibit team creativity and learning. For team members to feel comfortable speaking up with ideas or questions—an essential aspect of team learning—without fear of ridicule or punishment, all team members must work to create a climate of interpersonal safety. Otherwise, interpersonal risk is less likely to occur, particularly because the work is characterized by uncertainty and complexity.

One practical takeaway from the research on interpersonal safety is that a positive interpersonal climate is conducive to learning and creative performance under uncertainty, but it does not emerge naturally without the development of creative collaboration skills. Even when team members are embedded in a strong organizational culture, their perceptions of feeling safe to speak up, ask for help, or provide feedback tend to vary from team to team.[13] As we have indicated, team interpersonal safety is a shared belief that the team is safe for interpersonal risk taking. For the most part, this belief tends to be taken for granted and not given direct attention, either by individual team members or by the team as a whole.

Although implicit beliefs about interpersonal norms are sometimes explicitly discussed in a team, the act of them being made explicit does not in itself always alter the experience of team interpersonal safety. Team psychological or interpersonal safety is not to be confused with group cohesiveness, as research has shown that cohesiveness can reduce willingness to disagree and challenge others' views, such as in the phenomenon of the harmony facade and groupthink, which indicates a lack of interpersonal risk taking.

The terms *psychological safety* and *interpersonal safety* do not suggest careless permissiveness or an unrelentingly positive affect but rather a sense of constructive intent that the team will not embarrass, reject, or punish someone for speaking up with a divergent view. This sense of constructive intent increases with time as team members demonstrate mutual respect and trust through being vulnerable and actively supporting each other.

Perceptions of interpersonal safety should converge in a team, largely because these perceptions develop out of salient shared experiences among team members. For example, when a team experiences appreciation and interest in response to discussion of their own and others' mistakes, most members will conclude that making a mistake does not lead to rejection. Interpersonal safety can facilitate team learning work because it alleviates excessive concern about others' reactions to actions that have the potential for embarrassment or threat, which learning behaviors often have. For example, members may be unwilling to bring up errors that could help the team make subsequent changes because they are concerned about being seen as incompetent; this allows them to ignore or discount the negative consequences of their silence. In contrast, speaking up is more likely to happen when members respect and feel respected by other members and are confident that the team will not hold the error against them but instead support and help them.

More often than not, the performances of team members in an organization are assessed—whether frequently or infrequently, overtly or implicitly—in an ongoing way. The presence of team members with more power or status makes the threat of assessment especially salient, but it by no means disappears in the presence of peers and subordinates.

The salience of performance assessments can diminish interpersonal risk taking. There are specific risks to self-image among team members. When team members ask questions, seek information, admit or simply call attention to mistakes, ask for help, or accept the high probability of failure that comes with experimenting, they run the risk of being seen as incompetent. In the presence of supervisors and bosses, the risk of being seen as negative has been shown to be more acute among team members than it might otherwise be.

Psychological safety promotes low interpersonal risk and a climate of trust and mutual respect among team members, which provides the ground for such constructive interactions as care, concern, and spontaneous interpersonal coordination. Researchers have noted the role of psychological safety in promoting positive relationships in teams.

Because psychological safety facilitates attention, compassion, and concern for others, it enables close relationships among team members. Positive relationships are associated with a range of positive interpersonal outcomes, such as spontaneous interpersonal coordination and positive social exchange, suggesting that psychological safety is conducive to prosocial behavior through the positive interpersonal dynamics it engenders.[14]

Psychological safety encourages team members to focus on positive social exchange and open discussion of problems and issues.[15] It also provides a favorable environment for people to reconcile different goals and align their personal goals with those of the team. More directly, psychological safety gives rise to positive interpersonal relationships, which promote a sense of community, as well as identification with and psychological attachment to a group. Both a sense of community and group identification can enhance cooperative goal interdependence.

Current research suggests that active team support significantly influences collaborative behavior within teams, as well as deepens trust between team members.[16] The level of active support that team members experience from each other influences their own willingness to risk being vulnerable and deepens their commitment to the team project. Team members realize they cannot accomplish the creative project only through their own efforts, so they look for active supportive behavior from other team members, which encourages their own collaborative efforts and trust. Team members experience productive and creative relationships with each other when they feel valued by each other. Feeling supported and valued increases the willingness to invest even greater efforts and commitment to the creative project.

Understanding fear is an important task for those who want to effectively manage creative teams. We have found it valuable when working with creative teams to actively and openly discuss fears and the importance of psychological or interpersonal safety. The following quote seems appropriate for collaborative teams: "Feel the fear and do it anyway."

Team members need to become vulnerable and express their fears openly to each other. Doing so allows for the development of a supportive network for each team member. It is here that the leader of the team can model how to deal with fear triggered by the turbulence of creative collaboration.

Chapter Five

Failure

"Failure isn't a necessary evil. In fact, it isn't evil at all. It is a necessary consequence of doing something new."—Ed Catmull[1]

In our experiences with teams, we have found Catmull's framing on failure both accurate and helpful. But members of nascent teams will usually not ready to accept the fact that failure is a necessary, even healthy, consequence of teamwork. Not only is failure an everyday attribute of creative pursuits, but it is also a looming possibility around a team's raison d'être. This is particularly true for athletic teams (winning and losing), research and development, business, and even what we do—teaching visual storytelling. All of these team endeavors experience different types of failure, from constructively minor to destructively epic.

FAILURE AS A CONTRUCTIVE DEVICE

In television and film, there are generally three phases involved in creating a visual story:

1. Writing
2. Production
3. Editing

As failure is a necessary part of developing stories, each of these phases uses failure to cultivate story growth. In writing there is a read-through of the script, with constructive notes from those listening to it. The aim of this process is to honestly gauge the effectiveness of the story. Ed Catmull calls creative projects that he and his award-winning teams work on "ugly babies." He explains, "Candor is the key to collaborating effectively. . . . Pixar films are not good at first, and our job is to make them so—to go, as I say, 'from suck to not-suck.'"[2]

With such feedback, young writers must learn quickly that *they* are not *their ideas*. It takes experience to constructively hear feedback on an idea. This is because any note that questions the quality or effectiveness of a script idea feels like a failure.

Creators have to learn to separate their personal ownership and deep creative involvement in their ideas from the responses their ideas generate. Writers reduce ugliness and instill excellence in stories over multiple drafts and feedback sessions on a script. Creativity is a process.

The same is true during production, when "dailies" (raw footage) are screened after shooting and rough cuts are screened after first edits of the footage. Thick skin is in order for carefully hearing how a story is coming across. Creative excellence is not something that comes out immediately. It comes out with the dimension provided by constructive feedback.

The beautification process around collaborative projects can be seen as a series of responses to "microfailures." Out of the failures come improvements and impact in the story. But there are other failures (micro and otherwise) that build not only the creative products teams are working on but also the teams themselves. For instance, the best opportunities for team growth are gifts of Murphy's law. If something can go wrong, it will. And in creative collaboration, Murphy rules, and is a vital factor in determining whether a team will fall apart or use it as a basis for developing and actualizing their creative potential.

THE LOST CARD

In one TV production series, students experienced the nightmare of the digital age: a lost card. With the advent of digital technology, film stock and videotape have been replaced by small digital cards that store all of the shots and sounds acquired in production.

As show editor, Kate's job was to meticulously track and back up all video cards used for production. She would deliver a blank card to a camera operator and collect it after a scene was completed, replacing it with a new card for the next scene. Then she would transfer and duplicate all of the footage from the card onto a hard drive for editing and backup. Kate was very good at her job, and her teammates counted themselves lucky that she was their editor.

On the day after final episode was shot, one of the editors working with Kate realized that they were missing a card. It wasn't just any card; it was the card with the footage from the most complicated production elements they had shot as a team. This particular shoot involved five principal actors, multiple extras, a rented hall, rented chairs and tables, and catering for fifty people. In addition, there were several very complicated camera moves that, just by themselves, took hours to complete.

As a lost card is every production team's nightmare, the entire team of twenty students dispersed and covered every inch of territory on location and between and at the school—to no avail. The footage was forever lost, and unless they had some kind of a miracle up their collective sleeve, their finale was not to be.

Fortunately, this team had worked together long enough to know there was only one way to respond to this failure: Learn from the mistake, move on, and make it better. They immediately embraced Kate in a gesture of comradery because they knew how they would feel if they had lost the card, and they reminded her how important she was to the team. Then they recreated the final episode—called back the actors and the chairs and the tables and the food. They produced it better and in half the time of the first attempt, and the finale and series as a whole were great.

FAILING TOGETHER

Failure is a concrete part of creative collaboration that must first be accepted, and ultimately embraced. This is because failure coincides with group learning and the development of trust and interdependence. A team that allows for failure is a team ready to grow and succeed. Teams and their members must own their failures rather than running from or avoiding them. What we need to do if we want to learn from failure is create a culture grounded in constructive intent: promoting experimentation, reflection, and learning, as well as constructive criticism and collaboration.

Failure is an important force particularly at the inception of a creative team, when uncertainty runs high and vulnerability runs low.[3] Getting past the cultural programing and platitudes surrounding failure requires vulnerability in terms of an open discussion of this widely feared F-word.

From very early in most of our lives, *failure* is an emotionally loaded word connoting something bad as well as a sign of weakness. We fear the imagined negative consequences that follow the failure. This fear can lead to having low self-esteem, avoiding challenging tasks, and feeling pessimistic. Uncertainty is an ever-present hotbed for failure in a creative team. Constructively dealing with failure in a creative team requires a deep level of trust and interpersonal safety among team members, as we shall see.

It is unfortunate that so many organizations today have a culture of "perfection": a belief that failure is unacceptable. However, for teams doing creative work, a more useful motto is "If you fail to make mistakes, then you are not taking enough risk in your work."

Failure is a real event, especially when trying to do something creative that hasn't been done before. A team that allows for failure is a team ready to learn, grow, and succeed. Yes, failure is painful and hurts, but to develop real learning, the pain needs to be acknowledged while also embracing the failure as a wonderful opportunity to grow and learn. Failure, in reality, is inevitable and often out of our control, but an important driver of learning something new.

But fortunately, members of a creative team can choose to understand it, to learn from it, and to recover from it emotionally while collectively and actively supporting each other in the learning process. Systematic desensitization occurs when we own the failure and choose not to let it stop us from becoming courageous and taking risks. The motto for the team might be something like, "yeah, we failed, but it's a chance for us to learn a new and better way of doing something together.

The more we do this, the more the dysfunctional aspects of failure diminish. Embracing our failure is not only a sign of courage; it is also an opportunity for us to reach beyond the failure and harness that energy for learning and self-development. The idea of embracing failure is a great mind-set for making the most of feedback and increasing team members' resilience.

Experimentation is essential to creative collaboration, but it comes with the risk of failure. Encouraging risk taking involves helping team members not only to make sense out of failure but also to feel safe with failure.

Perceived failure has at least as important a role in our experience, education, and professional development as perceived success—if we learn from it. The experience of failure is not something to be avoided. Rather it needs to be viewed through the constructive lens of self-improvement so that the blow to a team member's self-image allows for resilience.

Researchers in the basic sciences realize that, although the experiments they conduct occasionally produce a spectacular result, a large percentage of them fail. How do these scientists keep from being overwhelmed with worry of failing? First, they know that failure is not optional in their work; it's part of being at the cutting edge of scientific discovery. Second, far more than most of us, they understand that every failure conveys useful insights. Life in creative teams can be viewed more like science in terms of embracing the concepts of trial and error because it is a necessary part of the creative process. As Thomas Edison stated, "I have not failed. I've just found 10,000 ways that won't work."

Members of a creative team can learn to embrace failure as something to learn from when experimenting with creative possibilities.[4] Imagine a spectrum among team members running from deep fears of failure to deep trust that failure will improve the creative output of the team. The higher the level of vulnerability-based trust in a team, the more creative and effective the team will be in collaborating together and creatively and constructively learn from failures.

Some current research in neuroscience demonstrates that at times we actually need to make mistakes in order to grow our skills and talents.[5] It has been discovered that the reward areas of the brain activate when people learn from their mistakes. Thus, while people normally feel bad about mistakes and try to avoid them in the future, the reality is that sometimes they need to make mistakes in order to improve. These neuroscientists have also found that, if people are provided the opportunity to reflect on mistakes, then they can actually feel good about them rather than ruminating on them. After reflecting positively on mistakes, we may not be so averse to trying something new. Insights from failure can be very rewarding, given time for reflection. Learning from failure can pave the way for highly creative teams.

Expending energy on preventing errors and mistakes tremendously thwarts and strangles the creative and collaborative process. In highly functioning creative teams, members are willing to openly talk about failures and what they learned from them. Failure is an important discussion topic in their team culture. Moving forward by learning from failure tends to distinguish creative teams from those who cannot collaboratively create.

When asked about mistakes, team members may focus on protecting their egos by brushing off the failure as "no big deal" or believing it wasn't their fault, but such distancing from failure may have adverse effects. Team members have both cognitive and emotional responses to their failures. However, the important thing to remember is not to avoid the emotional pain of failing but to use that pain to fuel improvement. Emotional responses to failure can hurt and feel awful. In order to avoid those emotions, people often choose to think self-protective thoughts after they make mistakes. However, it is clear from research that, if the focus is on the emotional hurt, then team members will put more effort into making sure they won't make the same type of mistake again.

Current research demonstrates that active team support significantly influences collaborative behavior within teams, encourages risk taking, and provides a safety net for failure.[6] The level of active support that team members experience from others influences their own willingness to being vulnerable and deepens their commitment to the team project.

Team members realize they cannot accomplish the creative project just through their individual efforts, so they look for active supportive behavior from other team members that encourages their own collaborative efforts and trust. Team members experience productive and creative relationships with each other when they feel valued by each other, even if they fail at some point in the creative project. Feeling supported and valued increases the willingness to invest even greater efforts and commitment to the creative project.

Without the fear-based bottled-up defensive energy, members are released to pour more of their energy into creative work together. When fear levels in a team are high, the creative collaborative process within the team is significantly impaired, as is learning from failures. Team members' energies are defensive rather than collaborative or creative. Creativity is severely restricted and greatly reduced. Perspectives are narrowed. Feelings and emotions become disruptive and disabling.

Learning from failure can pave the way for highly creative teams.[7] Tying up energy in striving for to prevent errors and mistakes thwarts and strangles the creative process. In highly creative teams, we have found that team members are willing to openly talk about failures and what they learned from them.

Failure is vitally important and discussable in team culture. Moving forward by learning from failure tends to be a distinguishing factor in effective creative teams.

Chapter Six

Authority

"If you want to hire great people and have them stay working for you, you have to let them make a lot of decisions, and you have to be run by ideas, not hierarchy."—Steve Jobs[1]

There is a paradox built into the leadership of a team. At a very basic level, high-functioning teams need a delicate blend of both dictatorship and democracy to succeed. Apple founder Steve Jobs was the embodiment of this paradox as a notoriously difficult, even cruel, boss to work for. And yet, because he listened to those around him, he was the architect of profound creative and collaborative accomplishments.

The concept of nonautocratic, even benevolent, dictatorship is by no means a new idea. The namesake furniture of King Arthur's mythical Knights of the Roundtable represents the concept of juxtaposing equality with nobility. Everyone at the roundtable was considered trustworthy and equal in these meetings. The concept of a roundtable meeting continues to be practiced in collaborative settings across the world today.

Authority is a word we use to describe this delicate dance between the human tendency to operate in hierarchical, top-down systems. When people operate in hierarchy over long periods of time, getting to the top becomes the conscious and unconscious objective of work rather than the work itself.

Hierarchy in collaborative settings is likely borne out of our basic foundations of upbringing. Our parents and teachers were, at least most of the time, our benevolent dictators or bosses who decided for us until we were old enough to decide for ourselves. Teachers take on a very similar role in formal education as dictators of essential (to them, at least) knowledge for our

51

proper upbringing. Because this hierarchy is so deeply ingrained, it is not only continued into the worlds of professional organizations but is also familiar and even comforting. It is seldom questioned or discussed.

So it is that life-informed experiences of authority are ripe with dysfunctional behavior, from fallible parents to ineffective teachers to rebellious children and disruptive students. Authority, and the power that goes with it, often has a seductive quality about it, with dangerous outcomes.

PREOCCUPATION WITH AUTHORITY

A few years ago, we had a show team that came up with one of the most creative and challenging production ideas we had ever seen. The team happened to have a couple of extraordinarily talented creators: one, a writer, and the other, a director. As is often the case when extraordinary talent rises up in a student environment, others in the creative team became sensitive to and increasingly envious of the compliments these two students were receiving in response to their work. Unknowingly to us, a few of them built a secret alliance against these two students—and also us, their authority figures. Envy is not necessarily a bad thing to feel in a team environment, as it can inspire better performances in peers. In this case, it was malicious.

This is an example of one type of preoccupation with authority: joining forces to eliminate authority. In our setting, it tends to happen with older, more experienced students who are close to the end of their education. They're often restless and looking to buck the bridle of the authority of the institution that binds them—especially when they are having problems performing well.

The thought process seems to be, "I've been here for almost four years, and I know this stuff. I don't need this old teacher telling me what is good and what is not good. It's time for me to demonstrate my abilities on my own. If I am not doing well, it's not my fault. It's my teacher's fault." Ironically, students who blame authority figures for their problems near the end of their studies probably need them even more. This is a form of scapegoating; "when members of a group are suddenly faced with uncertainty and ambiguity regarding direction, they unconsciously collude to dispel them by projecting them onto a leader role."[2] Because the efforts of this particular series idea became focused on the authority figure rather than the show idea, it did not take long for the entire project to unravel. In the end we held ourselves responsible for not realizing what was going on until it was too late.

When leaders lead by position—my way or the highway—all members of the team focus on and follow orders of the team leader. This is not only incredibly inefficient but also is a recipe for failure in collaborative undertakings.

Many professional leaders see this phenomenon in the form of *managing-up* tactics of intermediate managers who report to them. This happens when team members focus all of their efforts and achievements on impressing leaders above them in the hierarchy. The leaders they perform for see all of their best behaviors and outcomes. Those below or on the same level as these types of managers often see the worst behaviors and outcomes from them.

Career coach Curtis Odom advocates leading by influence as opposed to leading by authority:

> The best of leaders are even better followers. . . . Leadership is not telling others what to do. Leadership is inspiring others to do what needs to be done. A title alone does not make you a leader. Genuine leaders take a stand and motivate others to join them in a noble purpose. It is through the skills of influence that leadership works best.[3]

Actually, every team member is capable of evoking leadership by influencing some aspect of the creative project. The term "follower" is loaded and often viewed negatively by team members. In actuality every team member is responsible for leadership in terms of the creative project; they are all capable of influencing the development of the creative project.

This means finding the right space somewhere between autocrat and a committee. What is the difference between a highly functioning creative team and a committee? In semantic terms, there really is no difference. A committee is a collaborative gathering for a shared purpose. But committees, especially in academic circles, have a reputation for being a large collection of autocrats, often supporting nineteenth-century inventor Charles Kettering's eloquent warning "If you want to kill any idea in the world, get a committee working on it."

Ed Catmull provides some helpful suggestions for walking the line between these two extreme outcomes of collaboration:

Although we are a director- and producer-led meritocracy, which recognizes that talent is not spread equally among all people, we adhere to the following principles:

- Everyone must have the freedom to communicate with anyone. . . .
- It must be safe for everyone to offer ideas. . . .
- We must stay close to innovations happening in the academic community. . . .

We want everyone to question why we're doing something that doesn't seem to make sense to them.[4]

The key is open communication, along with a leader, or leaders, open to hearing that communication.

This is one way any team member can exert influence in shaping the development of the creative project. The key is a leader, or leaders, open to soliciting and hearing team members' perspectives on the creative project.

Author Leah Curtin draws a connection to quantum theory in considering how to reframe a gathering of individuals into a highly functioning team. She explains that, in an individual mind-set, group members seek order and stability and do their best to keep disorder at bay with clear boundaries and roles.

In a quantum (holistic) mind-set, boundaries and roles are seen as porous and changeable, therefore affording what she terms an "interconnectedness—the dynamic energy, the 'vibrations' of further potential." Such an approach to collaboration "emphasizes relationships and integration; it is holistic rather than particulate."[5]

CONSIDERING A NONHIERARCHICAL WORKING ENVIRONMENT

The title of a recent article, "First, Let's Fire All the Managers," indicates that something is afoot in terms of traditional hierarchical, authority-centered organizations.[6] Recently there have been experiments by several organizations to address the dysfunctions associated with the traditional hierarchical authority in contemporary workplaces. Holacracy and Teal organizations are examples of such experiments that attempt to shed the dysfunctions of hierarchy by creating largely self-governing, multidisciplined collaborative teams.[7]

Working through the fears and preoccupation with authority figures is necessary for a real sense of interdependence among members of a creative team. Attempting to work it through involves team members being vulnerable with their fears and authority issues impinging on the team. The uncertainty surrounding how authority figures will react is often quite high at the inception of a creative team and forms a basis for debilitating fears.

Much of the deference and obsequious behavior around authority figures is culturally programed at an early age. Continuing research on "obedience" to authority indicates how unlikely someone is to challenge an authority figure, even when what they are asked to do borders on the "unethical." With a deep fear of disapproval from an authority figure, it is not surprising that upward communications are so often distorted or avoided.

When an authority figure who has not been trained in creative collaboration team dynamics conducts a team meeting, more often than not they are likely to do at least 75 percent of the talking. Usually, team members at these meetings are paying the most attention to the reactions of the authority figure and addressing their comments to the authority figure rather than other team members.

This is not surprising. Typically, CEOs and other top-level managers went through the same schooling and cultural programing as members of their team. So, they themselves lack awareness of best team practices and the necessary skills for effective collaboration in creative teams.

ALTERNATIVE PRACTICES OF AUTHORITY

When the idea for the TV series *Breaking Bad* was pitched to Michael Lynton[8], CEO of Sony Entertainment, he responded: "Let me get this straight. It's about a high school chemistry teacher, middle-aged, children, he has cancer and he decide to go off to be a crystal meth dealer. That is the craziest and worst idea of a television show I have ever heard. And I don't care who writes it . . . that's nuts."

The person pitching the series responded: "We really believe in this, we really believe in Vince, and we feel this can be a really terrific show." At this point, Michael Lynton replied: "Hey guys, it your career. If you think it's that great you should go ahead with it." In a strictly hierarchical setting, the CEO's harsh criticism of the series would have ended the prospect of series. But this benevolent dictator's trust in his colleagues led to one of the most successful series in television history.

Through cultural programming, team members are often imbued with the existential script message of (1) doing whatever someone in authority wants, even though they disagree or have reservations about it, and (2) doing it without openly complaining and openly expressing salient emotions. Children learn that it is socially unacceptable to disagree with an authority figure and to remain silent. Later on, when they are adults, they look to authority figures to tell them what is meaningful in their work lives without much conscious thought and reflection. They learn to compete with their peers and focus on the authority figure's definition of what is really important. They mistakenly believe that there is nothing they can learn from their peers and that they cannot question or disagree with authority figures.

Because most people are not taught how to collaborate, especially creatively, it is not at all surprising that they show up in organizations without the necessary skills for creative collaboration. Milgram's studies on obedience to authority and cult groups attest to the primitive unreflective and unconscious compliance with an authority figure.[9]

Based on our experience consulting with teams of managers and executives involved in studying their own leadership processes, it seems quite easy to discern the quickness with which panic, anxiety, fear, terror, and confusion push team members into almost immediately attempting to appoint someone a team leader.[10] Team members generally seem to believe that such an action will eliminate all emotional turbulence.

What is particularly revealing in cases like this is that there is generally no discussion of why teams need a leader nor what the leader would do for the team. Most teams like this rapidly regress to a familiar, deeply embedded "invisible box" that feels safe.

It became clearer in further work with such teams that the immediate invention of a leader role was a culturally induced social defense for subduing and warding off unfamiliar feelings of chaos, panic, anxiety, fear, uncertainty, helplessness, ambivalence, and insecurity that were beginning to emerge in team members.

It was striking that team members were not able to openly discuss with each other what they were actually experiencing emotionally or intellectually. Their ritualistic invention of a leader role served as a social illusion that everything in the team's world was stable and under control. It was familiar and comfortable. The illusion masked over the anxiety, awkwardness, and fear of falling apart or being inadequate to control powerful forces both inside and outside themselves.

The invention of the leader role functioned as a form of social magic that allowed team members to narrow their fears and anxiety into one familiar place instead of diffusing it through what initially feels like a random and chaotic team environment. The creation of the leader role considerably reduced anxiety, terror, helplessness, and chaos—or so it seemed—but not without the team being unable to creatively develop as a collectivity or to develop their abilities and skills to constructively deal with their feelings. Using the leader role as a social defense resulted in a ritualistic structure where team members deskilled themselves in terms of emotions and mindfulness in their collective work. In this process, they never learned or developed collaborative or emotional skills as a team. They seemed mentally and emotionally sluggish, resulting in a flawed process of reality construction and an inability to be collectively creative.

Moreover, in just going through the motions, they were unable to learn from the underlying interpersonal issues in a constructive manner. When there is a rapid regression to a familiar "comfortable" box, there is zero learning from the experience together and no opportunity to help each other develop emotional and mindfulness skills for creative collaboration in a team. Because the leader illusion is undiscussable by team members, learning about the illusion of the role is outside immediate awareness and is constantly reinforced.

Paradoxically, because no learning or skill development takes place, there is a stronger pull toward the existing invisible-box social system, so that dysfunctions and difficulties in the team are viewed as personal failings of either certain members or the leader. As long as faults, mistakes, and imperfections can be attributed to the personal flaws or failings of team members or the leader, the dysfunctional aspects of the team's invisible box go unexamined. There is no possibility of evolution or metamorphosis for the team when this takes place.

Further, there is an invisible norm that asking or reflecting on what others on the team may be feeling is taboo. This is the way in which psychohistory and cultural programing can significantly influence collaborative team dynamics negatively, destructively, and unnecessarily.

Team members often want to please the authority figure while simultaneously believing their peers are competitors who have little to offer. In actuality, there are few places in society where a member of a creative team can learn the skills necessary for creative collaboration in a meaningful and constructive manner.

Without having been explicitly taught collaborative skills, it is not surprising that most team members carry over the orientation and mental map they learned in their early school experiences into the organizations or teams, where they become preoccupied with pleasing authority figures or avoiding criticism from them. They learn to put on a game face and become skilled at psyching out what an authority figure wants while being reluctant to challenge or criticize them for fear of falling from their good graces.

Working through the fears and preoccupation with authority figures in a creative team is necessary for a real sense of working interdependence to develop. It requires the establishment of an environment that is psychologically safe for team members to be vulnerable with what they are experiencing intellectually and emotionally during the evolution of the creative project. It reduces team members' fears and preoccupation with authority.

Preoccupation with authority is a powerful force at the start of a creative team. For creative collaboration to be optimal, existing research clearly indicates that all members need to be visible to each other, which means that they need to be vulnerable to openly expressing their personal perspectives about the project and team process. Remaining silent deadens the creative process and can lead to members being written off by other members as having nothing to contribute or being hostile, bored, or totally uncommitted. And the sad reality is that "silent" members may be caught up in a cultural invisible box that limits their participation, especially if they are from a different country than the majority of the team.

In order to have influence, a team member must find their voice and use it. One of the ways we have learned to deal with preoccupation with authority is to bring it into the awareness of the team members through their body language. For instance, they seem to be focused on looking to the authority figure in the room rather than to each other for creative ideas; they focus their eye contact on the authority figure and not on each other; they discount creative ideas from other team members. We then turn the collective team meeting over to team members.

Most collective decisions on a creative team are achieved through a provisional consensus process among members. Consensus is a decision through dialogue and discussion by all team members, with every member's perspective expressed and taken into account. Consensus is listening, responding, being open, seeking out differences, and dealing with them constructively. Consensus decision making makes clear that silence is not assent and promotes collective commitment.

Chapter Seven

Difference

"Two heads are better than one only if they contain different opinions."—
Kenneth Kaye[1]

One of the most overlooked aspects of creative collaboration is considering how we put teams together the way we do. In typical team formations, it comes down to either placing the best or most talented individuals on a team or simply leaving the selection process up to participating individuals. Beyond these two possibilities, especially in student group projects, there is little to no thought into why we put specific people on specific teams. In fact, often there is no real reason other than the fact that the individuals are there—enrolled in a class or employed by an organization. Unfortunately, there are problems with all of these methods:

- Putting the best people on a team
- Individuals deciding their own teams
- No consideration of why we put specific people on a team

When it comes to maximizing the results of creative collaboration, all of these approaches consciously or unconsciously ignore one of the greatest attributes of high-performing teams: differences.

SHIFTING GROUND IN COLLABORATIVE WORKPLACES

In his book *The Diversity Bonus: How Great Teams Pay Off in the Knowledge Economy*, social scientist Scott E. Page argues that the incredibly complex world we are in now is nothing like the world of our grandparents, especially when it comes to collaboration.[2] Collaboration used to be what he termed additive: A good team in a physically laborious workplace where people chopped, riveted, and built had the most and best choppers, riveters, and builders. According to the research Page has done, additive collaboration doesn't work nearly as well in current workplaces where people think, innovate, pour over data and reports, and try to come up with path-breaking new technologies: "If the problem is hard, if the task is difficult, the best team doesn't consist of the best individual performers."[3]

Page calls this a diversity bonus: a complex coming together of both cognitive difference (information, knowledge, heuristics, rules of thumb, causal models, frameworks) and identity difference (race, gender, ethnicity, sexual orientation, religion, physical ability). This shifts a team's frame of reference from who are the smartest and most talented people in the room, to "who are the people who have germane knowledge that might be able to add to our solution here."

Along the same lines, author Steven Johnson suggests the consistent performance advantage of diverse-minded groups over like-minded groups comes down to a simple idea: "It is the nature of a complex problem that there are angles of it you cannot see from one perspective."[4]

Although the advantage of differences between team members defies common sense in everyday practice, we have regularly confirmed its benefits in our experiences with storytelling teams. Talent is a double-edged sword: though it's good to have, it often leads to closemindedness, therefore limiting the possibilities of creative achievement. Generally speaking, the more *different* nascent team members are from each other and the less acquainted they are with each other beforehand, the more imaginative and effective they are likely to be as a creative team.

WHAT A DIFFERENCE A DIFFERENCE MAKES

In a newly formed creative team composed of a wide diversity of members, initially there is much uncertainty about how the differences will play out in their work together. We have found a number of misconceptions about how to constructively cope with and manage differences and divergent perspectives within a creative team. For example, there is a primary belief that harmony is necessary for creative collaboration—that is, conflict-free interaction among creative collaborators avoids what is viewed as time-wasting debates and dialogues about how to create something new. Actually, we discovered that quite the opposite is the reality.

Current research indicates that what are often labeled as conflicts are actually important differences and divergent perspectives that, when focused on a team's creative project, generate more creative ideas than can be found in a conflict-free or conflict-avoiding team.[5] For team members to learn to constructively deal with differences, they must remain vulnerable and open-minded to how the differences relate to the creative project.

Teams whose members are different in meaningful ways have a greater potential for collaborative creative work than teams whose members tend to be homogeneous.[6] The creativity of diverse teams, however, depends heavily on a culture that embraces vulnerability, psychological safety, trust, and active support. Diversity in teams creates a greater potential for conflict between divergent perspectives. Learning to openly and constructively deal with such conflict rather than suppressing it or forming cliques is necessary.

Diversity within a team can take many forms: age, gender, ethnicity, cultures, sexual orientations, disabilities, skills and abilities, and more. Diversity within a team is not limited to those attributes that are observable but also include such invisible characteristics as educational backgrounds, generations, learning styles, life experiences, social identities, and problem-solving abilities. Multiple categories of diversity within a creative team can positively influence the creative outcomes. A broader definition of *diversity* might better undergird the range it can take in a team. It can be broadly defined as any dimension that can be used to differentiate team members from one another.

Developing creative teams capable of creating something out of nothing can be accelerated by diversity. Diversity among team members enhances creativity because it encourages the search for novel perspectives and information. Being exposed to diversity can also change the way team members think and frame things as they take in other perspectives. This is not just wishful thinking; it is the conclusion drawn from years of research from organizational researchers, psychologists, sociologists, and cinematographers.

The key to comprehending the positive aspects of diversity on a team is recognition that members bring different information, experiences, opinions, skills, interests, and perspectives. However, when a creative team brainstorms and all members share ideas, there is a danger that members may begin to feel overwhelmed and take the easy way out. The creative project is reduced to something banal or unexceptional but easy to do. It is important for members to keep openly challenging themselves and each other to go outside the expected boundaries of the creative project they are working on. It is here that exploring the real differences between them can have a big payoff in creativity.

A series of recent studies at institutions ranging from Rutgers University to MIT's Sloan School of Management has rigorously analyzed the tangible outcomes of diversity in a workplace.[7] On almost every measure used, teams comprised of members from a variety of racial, ethnic, and cultural backgrounds function more effectively than teams that are homogenous or made up of members with similar backgrounds. Although researchers are still working to comprehend why and how, most seem to agree with the preliminary theory that diverse teams perform better in all dimensions because they bring a wide variety of perspectives, experiences, and attitudes to the team. Teams with greater diversity generate a unique dynamic that is more wide-ranging in scope, breadth, and depth and equips them to meaningfully handle complex problems and challenges.

Research findings are quite clear: Creative teams improve their performance when they include both men and woman. Gender mix consistently makes a difference in creative output. In a 2012 analysis of nearly 2,400 international companies, Credit Suisse found that those with at least one woman on the board tended to be the strongest performers.[8] The benefits of having both men and women on the team were especially apparent in tough operating conditions and attributed to more team diversity and a wider distribution of leadership skills.

However, most research on how diversity affects creativity in teams focuses only on the macro-demographics, of a team so it is not known exactly how a particular demographic translated into greater creativity. Demographics are simply social categories; divergent thinking is the real driver for creativity in a team.

Divergent thinking is a thinking process used to generate creative ideas. It typically occurs in a spontaneous, free-flowing, nonlinear way so that several ideas are generated in an emergent fashion. Convergent thinking, unlike divergent thinking, is systematic and logical in character. Convergent thinking is often quite useful in putting the creative ideas into production. Divergent thinking is a major factor in creative abrasion, where different perspectives and ideas are honed into something unique from the clashing ideas. Different demographics can lead to greater divergent thinking in a team, but it is individual thinking styles rubbing against each other that is the most important source of creativity in a team.

While initially team members may gravitate toward people who share their views, opinions, and backgrounds, it is important to shake things up by creating as much diversity as possible within the team, which also allows for greater creative abrasion. Putting together transdisciplinary teams where members bring different skill sets and experiences is more likely to be the type of environment where meaningful creative collaboration can evolve.

Workplace diversity research suggests that exciting new ideas are also often borne out of the clash of difference perspectives through creative abrasion. On the surface, this collision of different perspectives, worldviews, experiences, and attitudes ignite conflicts between team members. Learning how to constructively work through these conflicts is a crucial skill in creative collaboration.

Much research by organizational scientists, psychologists, sociologists, economists, and demographers indicate that socially diverse groups (those with a diversity of race, ethnicity, gender, and sexual orientation) tend to be more creative than homogenous teams.[9] In homogenous teams, members tend to have the same blind spots and the same perspectives that seriously dampen collective creativity. This is not only because people with different backgrounds and experiences bring new information. Simply interacting with team members who are different pushes members to prepare, to anticipate alternative viewpoints, and to expect that reaching a consensus on a creative project will take some effort. Diversity of expertise and experience can offer advantages that sometimes are not apparent until members begin to collaborate.

Some research has shown that social diversity (age, race, ethnicity, gender, culture, sexual orientation) in a team can lead to discomfort, awkward interactions, mistrust, greater perceived interpersonal conflict, lower communication, less commitment, and more concern with being disrespected.[10] However, in terms of positive qualities, diversity encourages the search for novel information and perspectives that lead to more creative output. What is vital for diversity to enhance creativity in a team is a culture that promotes psychological safety, as well as real interdependence among members of the team rather than an individualistic culture.

Members of a homogeneous creative team rest somewhat assured that they will agree with one another, that they will understand one another's perspectives, and that they will be able to easily come to a consensus on their creative project. But when members of a group notice their differences—social, informational, and skills—they change their expectations. They anticipate differences of opinions and perspectives. They tend to assume it will be more difficult to arrive at a collective consensus on the shape and nature of a meaningful creative project. However, through the process of creative abrasion, they are much more likely to develop out-of-the-box ideas. Leaders who manage creative teams can make use of the undercurrent of diversity by designing a diverse team with the relevant dimensions suggested here, as well as realizing that creative abrasion will be operating at full tilt.

Part III

Conflict

Heaven is also a place where young screenwriters find themselves when they do not embrace conflict in creating their stories. Unfortunately, Heaven is not, as a rule, the best place for screenwriters to be.

The song "Heaven" by the Talking Heads tells the story of a perfect bar in heaven where the band plays your favorite song all night long. Heaven is not normally considered to be a problem, but in the circles of storytelling and creative collaboration, it is a significant problem. This is because nothing can really happen unless there is the possibility of it going wrong. Just like high-performance teamwork, good stories have no guarantees.

Beginning screenwriters learn very early in their training how to use conflict to make more interesting characters and more engaging plotlines. Even though they know what conflict is, they need to relearn it as storytellers because we are brought up to largely steer clear of conflict in our everyday lives. It carries a largely negative connotation.

Young writers unconsciously bring this conflict aversion into their story process when they create characters—imaginary beings whom they learn to love like their own children. Just try telling a first-time writer that you think they need to make some improvements on their protagonist when you read through the first draft of their script. Like parents, they protect their "children" by extending their everyday aversion of conflict to them and the stories around them—conflicts like contradictions in character, problems, challenges, questions, and threats to their static existence.

The same applies to the plots they first write. Plotlines in their first drafts happen with effortless ease: step 1, step 2, step 3, no problems, and easy outcomes. Quoting the Talking Heads, "It's hard to imagine that nothing at all [Heaven] can be so exciting" because, in stories, it is not.

CONTEXTS OF CONFLICT

Though there is conflict in everyday life, it is spread out over a broad span of time and really is more of an exception than a rule for most social interactions. In storytelling, conflict is exaggerated because stories are highly condensed and have limited temporal frames. Storytellers must deliver their goods in a matter of minutes. Thus, to make stories happen, writers need conflict.

Though not as concentrated as stories, time frames for creative collaboration are also more comparatively limited and, for many of the same reasons as stories, need conflict to create action, change, and growth. In this sense, conflict is an accelerant for action.

It is not uncommon for creative teams to start out in a heavenlike state as they get to know each other. About the time when they can talk about how they feel with each other, they usually begin to get restless and nervous because they have to get something done as a group. They have to make something happen. And as we've discussed, heaven is a place where nothing ever happens. The team needs to do something: in particular, take risks (action) and experience creative abrasion (reaction) together as they approach a shared goal.

There is a difference between external and internal conflict in a team. Internal conflict for team members is the conflict they feel about expressing different ideas and emotions to the team. For creative abrasion, each team member must be willing to risk disagreeing with someone on the team. This is often their worst fear and the basis of the inner conflict: being authentic or stifling one's self and holding back.

Being authentic promotes self-affirmation, while holding back contributes to a low self-image. On entering a creative team, most members fear conflict with other members of the team. Yet, somewhat paradoxically, conflict can often generate ideas for the creative project.[1] Often the best ideas arise out of great conflict. If everyone agreed all the time, there would be no reason to consider different perspectives or look for new ways to handle difficult situations.

Without any attempt to develop constructive ways of dealing with such conflict, many team members suppress or repress their suggestions, disagreements, comments, feelings, and perspectives. When this occurs, the team becomes void of both liveliness and creative ideas rather quickly. This internal conflict in the mind of individual members is a form of cognitive dissonance, where an individual holds inconsistent or opposing perceptions or beliefs. However, the fears are not usually tested to determine if they are only imagined or actually have a basis in reality. This is why constructive intent and building a climate of psychological or interpersonal safety is so crucial in developing a creative team. It is a safety net for members to take the risk of finding out what is real and what is imagined.

In actuality, one of the first moves away from singularity is for team members to take risks and begin to voice different perspectives from the one being discussed in the team. This is the only way out of the deadness of withholding conflicting viewpoints. A creative team being able to discuss perceived conflicts within a team actually provides each member a voice to influence the direction that the team takes in evolving the creative project.

When perceived conflicts are ignored or avoided rather than handled in a productive way, things are likely to stay the same or worsen. When team members express their differences and work through them, the ground is set for positive change to occur within the team. Moreover, when members of a team persevere through a struggle together and come out better on the other side, they realize the conflict has been worth it. Because the conflict is a shared experience, it likely increases trust and confidence among all team members.

Conflict needs to be engaged and constructively dealt with to build the character of the creative team and its individual members. It can foster the creativity of a team only when members acknowledge and are open to differences, engage in constructive conversations, take the perspectives of others into account, and learn to provide reflective summaries of each other's perspectives.

Engaged empathetic communication with a constructive intent is everything when it comes to finding a creative resolution, and it is where individual members learn to constructively handle conflict in order to harness and improve the team's creative potential. When conflict is constructively dealt with, it inspires all members to be part of the larger purpose of their project. The only way to break free of a negative dynamic in a team is to take a risk and confront it, and learn from it. Establishing team norms to deal constructively with conflicts and disagreement can be very useful in developing a creative team. [2]

Chapter Eight

Risk

"Risk is an influence affecting strategy caused by an incentive or condition that inhibits transformation to quality excellence."—Victor Elias[1]

Risk, like all other forces of creative collaboration, is not a one-step, switch-flicking process. It must be continually exercised in the beginning, middle, and end of the collaborative process. Risk is the art of initiating action in the context of uncertainty—making decisions that might be wrong. Risk requires both independent and collective courage to step forward into unknowns with very little to no clarity about resulting consequences. This is the nature of the creative process: We simply do not know if it will come out OK. But nothing can happen without risk.

One of the most telling examples of risk in creative storytelling occurs near the end of the creative process, when the editor brings the first cut of a scene. Even though the deadline and ultimate end of the project is drawing near, the risks feel as heavy as the first steps in the screenwriting process. Editors are always very nervous as they fiddle with wires and hard drives and computers used in the screening. And without fail, they feel the need to qualify what everyone is about to see. Everyone in the room is fully aware of the fact they are about to watch a rough cut, but the editor invariably adds a few more "roughs" to the equation: "I just want you to know this is really a rough, rough, rough cut. The sound isn't finished, and we're missing a couple of shots halfway into the scene, and the software was very buggy when I was applying transitions." Like so many other steps in creative collaboration, risk is scary but necessary. It builds creative and collaborative muscle for a team.

And every team needs a lot of this muscle because creative collaboration is really the coming together of thousands of decisions: some shared, some autonomous, but all of them attached to the constant threat of failure. Risks can and mostly do lead to success but not without the chance of being wrong and ultimately failing, and that in itself is OK.

AVOIDING RISK

One of the best ways to see the complex decision-making process around risk is to consider what teamwork looks like without it. The concepts of group-think[2] and the so-called Abilene Paradox[3] highlight the dysfunctional ways teams suppress divergent viewpoints and too quickly focus on convergence out of fear of dealing openly with conflict between members. They demonstrate quite clearly the absence of risk taking in creative teams.

Team members fear voicing their reservations and disagreement, which significantly undermines establishing real interdependence within the team. Risk taking among members is vital for establishing and developing real interdependence.

The Abilene Paradox was developed in a 1974 article by Jerry Harvey.[4] The name of the concept comes from an anecdote that he uses in his article to discuss the paradox: A family is playing dominoes on a porch on a summer night, when one of them suddenly suggests they take a trip to Abilene for dinner. Abilene is fifty-three miles away. The rest of the family indicate that they feel this is a great idea. The drive is a long one in stifling heat. When they get to the diner, the food is lousy. En masse, they leave the diner, and four hours later, they arrive at home. One of them says it was a great trip, to which another member states that they would have preferred staying on the porch. As they talk about it, each of them indicates they really did not want to go but did so because they thought everyone else wanted to go. Therefore, the trip to Abilene was actually a trip none of them wanted to take. The paradox is that none of them wanted to go, yet all of them agreed to go.

Each person did not want to rock the boat, so together they created a harmony facade.[5] While often the paradox is seen as an inability of the family to manage agreement, it really demonstrates an inability to manage disagreement because no one was willing to disagree about the decision to go to Abilene. They didn't really want to go but were afraid to voice the dissent openly. They all ended up regretting not speaking up in time. They seemed fearful of creative abrasion.

Similarly, groupthink illustrates team chemistry at its worst. When a team is caught in groupthink, it attempts to present an image of harmony and results in an irrational or dysfunctional outcome. Divergent and alternative points of view are actively suppressed and discouraged. Team members avoid raising debatable or controversial issues or alternative possibilities. This results in the loss of individual and team creativity, uniqueness, and critical thinking.

From the standpoint of groupthink and the Abilene Paradox, there are various ways that teams discourage risk taking and allowing and working through divergent points of view and disagreements:

1. Team members express a different opinion in meetings and offer a different opinion outside the meeting.
2. Team members are discouraged from dissenting, which is viewed as a lack of commitment.
3. Team members feel envy or resentment toward other team members.
4. Team members avoid responsibility and blame other team members.
5. Team members distrust each other.

Open expression of divergent perspectives and disagreements are useful for creative collaboration in creative teams. How to constructively handle divergent perspectives and learning what to do with disagreements that usually stay underground is vital for creative teams. Team members' fears about voicing divergent perspectives and conflicts need to be openly dealt with constructively and skillfully. As a team evolves members begin to realize that sometimes they have very different perspectives and emotions.

In fact, divergence and diversity are key components in generating creative ideas, provided the process is dealt with constructively and interpersonal safety has been established. Without a feeling of psychological safety, a conflict can feel like a failure and be frustrating to team members, even though differences in perspectives are a fundamental reason for creative teamwork. If members of a creative team actually agreed on everything, then working together would be relatively pointless.

In the phase where team members become aware of their differences, there can be strong feelings of frustration, anger, rejection, disappointment, and being overwhelmed by so many different perspectives. This type of turbulence in a team often feels chaotic. During this stage of development, creative team members are discovering how the team can constructively handle perceived conflicts with each other.

Team members are often reluctant to openly discuss their feelings and thoughts about opposing perspectives with each other. They don't directly or openly express it. Every creative team needs members who can help the team by challenging the tendency to smooth over divergent perspectives or to quickly adopt a viewpoint without critically reflecting on it simply to avoid disagreement. This stifles creativity and learning.

Sometimes lone dissenters are those who stand back and say, "Why are we even doing this? What if we looked at the thing laterally or turned it inside out or upside down?" The perceived dissenter opens up more ideas, and that often make for more originality. In many cases, the competitive conflict is actually just divergent thinking: a source of great creativity. Dissenters are the individuals who are often more willing to risk articulating the things that nobody else is willing to articulate. In the process of dissenting, they can raise the level of anxiety for other team members, which actually might contribute to more creative thinking within the team.

Existing research indicates that exposure to minority divergent perspectives within a team actually serves to stimulate team members to search for more information and to examine the information in more divergent ways, which enables the team to think more creatively as well as generate more creative solutions.[6] Minority views within a team do more than just diminish the negative impact of concurrence seeking such as groupthink or the Abilene Paradox.

Minority views within a team more often than not stimulates all team members to think in more divergent ways. It seems clear that minority dissent and divergence fosters conflict within the team. Minority views tend to give birth to emotional feelings of stress, anger, and irritation. However, this is a form of conflict while uncomfortable is healthy for the team when there is constructive intent within the team. It can lead to breakthrough creative ideas when team members openly and authentically express different perspectives. It is what we label creative abrasion. It is how creative abrasion works to polish the creative project of the team.

Research clearly demonstrates that a small minority of at least two people can change the team trajectory when the majority consistently embraces and champions their perspectives.[7] There is also research suggesting that dissent can help drive creativity. Charlan Nemeth, Berkeley professor, has researched the relationship between conflict and creativity for more twenty years. She has discovered that simply observing someone engaged in an act of dissent emboldens others to express their disagreements and break away from a majority viewpoint.[8]

In general, lack of dissent and disagreement is not a constructive outcome in a creative team. It is most likely a symptom of groupthink or harmony facade: when a team suppresses and denies differences in perspectives, especially strong disagreements or reservations, as well as emotional negativity. The facade is a public myth that members of the team are a harmonious social group with no real intellectual differences, emotional negativity, or unacknowledged and unresolved conflicts. Team members tend to describe the team in glowing terms, stressing only positive attributes—real, imagined, and those they wish were present—while simultaneously disclaiming the existence of any tensions or negativity.

Risk is the art of making decisions regardless of uncertainty—it is a decision that could very well turn out be wrong. The decision to risk is the courage to step forward into some unknown without being clear about the consequences or outcomes. However, it really is the only way for any team member to find out if other members can be trusted and whether it is psychologically safe to openly express disagreements and divergent thoughts and feelings. Taking risks within a creative team is the first step in establishing trust and psychological safety.

Risk taking by team members is any conscious or unconscious behavior in spite of perceived uncertainty about the action's outcome; possible benefits; or physical, economic, or psychosocial costs for themselves or others. Psychological safety is a shared belief that the team is safe for interpersonal risk taking. However, it can't exist without team members taking risks and experiencing the outcome.

When psychological safety has been established in a team, members feel free to be vulnerable and express themselves without fear of negative consequences for their self-image or career. In psychologically safe teams, team members feel accepted and respected. However, it is important to remember that they had to take the risk of being vulnerable to find out that it actually was safe to do so.

Risk taking by team members requires courage to make a choice and a willingness to confront whatever transpires. Courage is what is necessary for an interpersonal risk when the outcome is uncertain. A team member discloses something they previously would not have because it would make them too vulnerable. Research indicates that self-disclosure of vulnerable information is reciprocal; others tend to match the level of self-disclosure. Taking a risk activates vulnerability and sets the stage for developing trust among members and discovering how the team collectively enhances the creativity.

Paradoxically, a climate of psychological safety and trust can only be established when members take the risk of being vulnerable with each other. At first the outcome is uncertain because it has not been established how other members will respond to perceived risky actions and disclosures. Actions always have precedence over words; claiming it is safe to be open and vulnerable is different from being open and vulnerable and experiencing the resulting reaction of other team members. Without initial interpersonal risk taking, there can be no sense of psychological safety or trust. [9]

Aside from discussing the importance of acknowledging fears and how to constructively handle failure, managers can actively encourage members of the team to experiment with taking risks in their creative work together. One of the best ways for them to do this is to model what it is like to acknowledge fears and failures and take a risk.

Chapter Nine

Abrasion

"There is a need to recognize the very real opportunities and energies available when the heat and friction of abrading points of view are encountered. As in the great supercolliders used in the research of particle physics, it is precisely the managed collision of powerfully oppositional streams that releases previously untapped matter and energy."—Jerry Hirshberg [1]

Abrasion is the process of scraping or wearing something away.[2] Jerry Hirshberg coined *creative abrasion* to describe the turbulence among individuals of a group that is necessary for them to accomplish complex creative goals. What is being worn away in this type of abrasion are surfaces of individuality, to open up the shining core of collaborative potentials.

Creative abrasion "does not always erupt from a single triggering event. It can also do its work like the infinitesimal friction of water in a creek, forging its own course and, in crime, carving grand canyons."[3] It also does not usually happen immediately in a team formation. We see creative abrasion surface in the creative teams we work with as deadlines approach: script deadlines, shooting deadlines, editing deadlines, screening deadlines, award submission deadlines. A concrete deadline in a team is a recipe for creative abrasion. This is because they have to get something done together.

The ropes course exercise Amoeba Race comes to mind in conceptualizing creative abrasion in practice. In the exercise, a large group of individuals stand close together and are bound together with a large rope. The facilitator then tells the group to go pick up a ball on the far side of the field from their location as quickly as they can.

In order to accomplish this goal, these bound individuals must crash into each other, trip over each other, disagree, and maybe even fight with each other to get anything done together. And they will not accomplish their objective unless they ultimately learn to walk together.

The creative abrasion stage of collaboration is where the heavy lifting of working together happens. It is volatile and sometimes dangerous, even destructive, thus the continual risk in the process. But based on our experiences, it also is necessary for creative and innovative outcomes.

Many teams in entertainment media call this stage the "crunch." It's like an all-nighter before a project is due. As a deadline looms closer, the time frame to get the work done shrinks, therefore elevating the stress and adrenaline of the participants as their homeostasis is disrupted. This is the very ground where some of the most fascinating team accomplishments are realized.

POLISHING STONES

The concept of creative abrasion comes from a story Steve Jobs told about an early childhood experience, when an older neighbor invited him to help collect rocks and then took them into his garage, put them in a large canister with some gritted substance, and turned the motor on. There was quite a bit of noise as the stones rubbed up against each other and pounded around in the canister.

The next day, Steve and his friend open the canister, and he was amazed. The stones were now polished and shining in their beauty. He never forgot this experience, and he applied it to the development of creative teams: "It's . . . through that group of incredibly talented people bumping up against each other, having arguments, having fights sometimes, making some noise, and working together they polish each other and they polish the ideas, and what comes out are these really beautiful stones."[4] Creative abrasion at its best polishes very rough ideas into beautiful new gems.

Linda Hill of the Harvard Business School, Greg Brandeau of Pixar and Walt Disney, Emily Truelove of the MIT Sloan School of Management, and executive Kent Lineback authored a book called *Collective Genus*, in which they discuss the importance of creative abrasion, creative agility, and creative resolution for creative teams.[5] Creative abrasion happens with passionate, energized, yet healthy discussions that generate an array of ideas. Team members realize that seldom do they get creative or out-of-the-box thinking without engaging energetically with diverse thoughts.

Creative agility means that team members quickly reflect, offer reactions and alternatives, and refine various ideas in a meaningful way. It is a constant process of exploring ideas as they unfold over time and allowing meaningful changes to occur.

Creative resolution is when team members can constructively combine or reconfigure diverse ideas, even if they seem to be in opposition. They learn along the way that they don't give in, simply to get along with other members. They know how energy lights up the room when they are collectively onboard with the way their project unfolds.

The key issue with divergent perspectives within a creative team is members being able to openly express divergent views without rejection or to disagree with another member without fear of hurting them or receiving defensive responses. Often the most important teamwork happens in the least comfortable spaces.

However, while divergent perspectives might feel risky and confrontational, especially when awkward facts or dilemmas are brought up, they can actually improve how members relate to each other and provide a more creative twist on their work.

Bringing up difficult issues to the team often feels awkward and uncomfortable; team members often don't want to upset other members. These uneasy feelings usually have less to do with other team members and more to do with unconscious anxiety about being able to handle difficult conversations effectively. Overcoming such anxieties and having the difficult conversations often feels like a challenge, yet it is necessary. These kinds of conversations require team members to operate outside their usual comfort zones.

Members need to remember that doing things in the same way will produce the same results. It takes a shift in mind-set from seeing difficult conversations about divergent perspectives as a hurdle to seeing them as useful for increasing the creativity of a project. A difficult conversation about different perspective can deepen trust within the team.

Team members have to be very aware of the indirect comments, conversations, and body language within the team. If a team member sees people who are threatened by any revision or are unhappy about one element of their project, they need to step up and say, "Look, I sense that a couple of us don't feel committed to the revision or the way we are operating, so let's continue to talk this out as a team. I think this conversation will help build the levels of trust and openness among us."

Most of us will likely recognize this common dilemma in a traditional team meeting: You are in a meeting of ten members. An important issue is brought up for discussion. An inner circle of three members discuss possible solutions about how to proceed, while the other seven members say nothing, and none of the three asks them for their viewpoints.

The seven members feel they are being left out of the discussion, and they leave the meeting without the slightest commitment to the decisions made by the dominant three. They start shadow meetings in small groups after the meeting. "Lousy ideas and decision were made," they say. When the three actives team members hear about these discussions, they are genuinely amazed: "We had a meeting about this! Why didn't they say anything?"

In the follow-up meeting, the three active team members shoot down the suggestions presented by the seven. The seven people basically lose their voices and shut up while remaining uncommitted to the project. Now, the three most outspoken members dominate the discussion, regardless of the actual value of their input. They feel very motivated and engaged with the illusionary "consensus" decision.

TYPES OF CONFLICT

There are three areas where conflict can occur in a team: task, interpersonal relationships, and process for achieving the task. Task or cognitive conflict is disagreement over ideas, viewpoints, and opinions pertaining to the team's task. In contrast, relationship conflict is disagreement resulting from interpersonal incompatibilities, which includes such affective components as feeling tension and friction. Process conflict is conflict about finding meaningful ways to divide and delegate responsibility and deciding how to get work done in a fast but high-quality manner. Each of these areas of conflict results in different team dynamics, but very little is known about strategies teams employ to manage conflict or the efficacy of these strategies.

When team members are able to integrate ideas across functional areas and when team interests are placed above individual functional interests, the potential for creative problem solving is greatly enhanced. Rather than individuals generating creative ideas guided by their disciplinary perspectives and self-interests, the idea-building process occurs freely and from a variety of perspectives, where each functional specialty builds on the best ideas of the other. Instead of a rigid hierarchical structure, with each team member assigned a specific role where they are expected to remain, multidisciplinary teams are more organic, with members taking on different roles according to the changing needs of the creative project. Team members take risks by venturing out of their more comfortable specialization areas into situations where they may not be as sure of what they are doing and where their roles are not as well defined.

This can require greater effort on the part of members and the team because it can be more difficult to achieve a creative synthesis of many perspectives than it is for each member to focus solely on their own perspective. It requires members to think in new and more collaborative manner. Often it is differences in team members' perspectives that enables a team to operate with more of the razor's edge needed to create new projects. The challenge a team faces is to create a productive level of conflict that enhances their collective level of creativity.

For an effective creative process within a creative team, there needs to be both out-of-the-box ideas and critical thinking. These two rather different styles of thinking are usually referred to as divergent thinking (free-floating ideas) and convergent thinking (critical thinking). The divergent thinking modality encourages team members to free associate and encourages out-of-the-box ideas, while the convergent thinking is activated to figure out what divergent ideas are relevant and worth acting on further.

Divergent thinking generates a variety of ideas about the creative project. Convergent thinking then follows with disclosure and advocacy of ideas. Members must make their ideas explicit and develop a rationale for them. Disclosure and advocacy can be contentious in terms of the variety and range of ideas generated. Convergence requires resolution of differences and a commitment to a course of action. When a team converges on an idea or course of action, it can move to execution. Creative abrasion is not something that just happens at the beginning of a creative project. It can occur anytime the team faces a problem or opportunity that requires collective rather than individual action.

Nonverbal cues and direct interpersonal contact are quite important in the transmission of emotions related to conflicts in teams. Emotional moods tend to fluctuate as a creative team unfolds. Often the group mood can be identified by a high-energy expression of emotions from a single team member who voices the underlying mood felt by others who do not have high energy and are not as emotionally expressive.

One danger with creative abrasion is stifling creativity. Moving into convergent thinking too quickly throws a wet blanket on team members' creative fire. Even though a team member may accept that one of their ideas is not workable or relevant, when the idea is criticized or disregarded, their creative enthusiasm deflates, and their future contributions can be deeply stifled.

In organizations with high-performing and creative teams, it is important to build norms around conflict. It must be seen as important and openly dealt with in a supportive, constructive manner.

Part IV

Interdependence

"It is not the similarity or dissimilarity of individuals that constitutes a group, but interdependence of fate."—Kurt Lewin[1]

Interdependence is mutual reliance on each other. It is a real connected mind-set of all individuals in a team. Interdependence means that one member's actions will affect other members, as well as the state of the team. It is a process in which interacting members of a group influence one another's experiences, thoughts, and emotions.

It is the connected mind-set in action. Interdependence approaches work from the standpoint that any team member's success depends on the performances of those around them. It's like a 360-degree trust fall: If someone needs me, I will catch them; if I need help from others, I will be caught before I hit the ground.

THE EMERGENCE OF INTERDEPENDENCE IN TEAMS

When talking about singularity of individual states that members bring to their teams, we found a helpful parallel in chaos theory to make sense of dynamics in collaborative environments. We have regularly observed a close association between singularity and the chaos theory concept of "sensitivity to initial conditions." This suggests that every collaborative experience is different because participating individuals are nearly infinitely different from one another. Because of this, teamwork can be as unpredictable as the weather.

But as chaos theory pioneer Edward Lorenz explains, persistent examinations of chaotic behaviors, like the weather, will ultimately reveal order and patterns.[2] The emergence of interdependence in creative collaboration environments is an example of order in the often-chaotic process of teamwork. It is the point at which a group of individuals transforms into a team.

If we think of creative collaboration as a pot of water on a stovetop, then interdependence is the point when the water boils. But just like the adage "A watched pot never boils," interdependence does not emerge in predictable or easily observable ways. As a rule, the phrase is meant more as an example of psychological time, or, how time feels when you want something to happen sooner.

The principle of quantum theory used to describe this waiting game is the Quantum Zeno Effect, a paradoxical outcome of scientific measurement first described by scientist Alan Turing.[3] The Quantum Zeno Effect suggests that observations of phenomena—in our case, the dynamic process of creative collaboration—can affect the phenomena in a negative or positive manner. In the case of the watched pot, this would imply that watching the pot could actually have an effect on its boiling process.

In the context of complex systems, the Quantum Zeno Effect derives from the reality that everything in the universe behaves like both a particle and a wave. Therefore, watching a pot boil as a particle is not a complete or accurate frame of reference. Similarly, waiting for a group of individuals to suddenly become a team is not an observable outcome because it is a dynamic, wavelike phenomenon. This is why we find it difficult to frame the practice of creative collaboration in terms of simple steps and precise outcomes. Like the weather, we can expect basic patterns and outcomes and even some degree of short-term predictability but always with a degree of impreciseness and sometimes unexpected results.

But in most creative collaboration settings that we have observed, interdependence, like a boiling pot of water, eventually emerges out of the chaos of colliding individuals. In the following chapters, we examine the emerging features of interdependence—chemistry, commitment, empathy, trust, and resilience—and their respective forces at play in the complex process of creative collaboration.

Chapter Ten

Chemistry

"Chance favors the connected mind."—Steven Johnson [1]

Coach Mike Krzyzewski, the all-time winningest coach in Division I college basketball, subscribes to a simple theory in building chemistry with the teams he works with. It's called the metaphor of the fist: "With a basketball team, it just works out. I coach a team where there are five guys. And if five can play as one, that means you're constantly going at people with all the talents of the team that you have." [2] Chance certainly has favored Coach K in building a connected mind-set on his teams. In addition to combining talents, learning to bond and play as one also creates the possibility for serendipitous breakthrough: a whole that is even greater than the sum of the parts.

In his book *Where Good Ideas Come From*, Steven Johnson calls attention to the power of colliding hunches. Hunches around creativity and innovation, lurking in one person's mind, need to collide with other hunches lurking in someone else's mind. Thus a sensible task is to create ways for hunches to come together and turn into something bigger. "That's why," Johnson notes, "the coffeehouse in the age of the Enlightenment or the Parisian salons of modernism were such engines of creativity because they created a space where ideas could mingle and swap and create new forms." [3]

ARISTOTLE AND THE CONNECTED MIND

In 2012, Google created a research project: "Code-named Project Aristotle— a tribute to Aristotle's quote, 'the whole is greater than the sum of its parts' (as the Google researchers believed employees can do more working together than alone)."[4] The project investigated the characteristics of more than 180 high-performing Google teams and interviewed hundreds of employees to find the components that would allow the creation of "dream teams" for collaboration.[5] The researchers originally thought they would uncover the optimal mix of individual personality characteristics and skills necessary for establishing a highly performing creative team. To their surprise, the best team practices they discovered had very little to do with individual personality characteristics and skills.

It turned out that the most important factor involved in high-performing teams was the way in which team members interacted with each other when collaborating, as well as how they structured their collaborative work with each other. In high-performing teams, there was an amazing equivalency in how much time each person spoke during their collective meetings. Moreover, the distribution of "talk time" appeared to happen in a flowing manner, where there was no need for anyone to monitor or control the ongoing dialogue. By the end of the project, every team member seemed to have roughly spoken the same amount of time in meetings. The research also indicated that, if one team member or a small clique of the team spoke most of the time, then the collective intelligence of the team declined. There were no invisible or silent members in the high-performing teams.

The second factor uncovered by the researchers was that, in the high-performing teams, members seemed to demonstrate high levels of interpersonal or social sensitivity. This consisted largely of members being skilled at recognizing how team members felt based on tone of voice, facial expressions, body language, and other nonverbal cues.

Additionally, psychological safety existed on high-performing teams, where members felt they were able to take risks and be vulnerable in front of each other; they could openly discuss both their perspectives and feelings about working together. Google's finding is consistent with other research on the effects of psychological safety on a team's creative performance.[6] It is quite clear that feelings of psychological safety directly affect the involvement, engagement, and vitality of members in doing creative work together. The fact that all members of the team expressed themselves almost equally in itself testifies to the establishment of a culture of psychological safety in these teams.

The Google study provides insight into the chemistry that exists in creative teams that excel. Team chemistry is the dynamic that arises from the different qualities each member contributes and the interactions of members with each other as the creative project evolves.

DEFINITION OF *TEAM CHEMISTRY*

Team chemistry is one of the most complicated factors in developing a high-performing creative team. Creative teams are much more than just a collection of talented team members. In order to collaborate, a creative team has to be able to combine the efforts and abilities of members in a way that promotes synergy. In some ways, it is the nascent state of interdependence propelled by the early incidents of abrasion. The hope with team chemistry is the achievement of a gestalt or symbiosis where the whole of the team is greater than the sum of its individual members. But initially the reality is uncertain.

Team chemistry in action is also reflected in the collective emotional mood that more often than not fluctuates as the creative project takes shape. Team emotional mood involves specific emotional states, such as fear or euphoria or dread. It also involves more diffuse feeling states, such as negativity and positivity. Team members are often not aware of how their collective emotional mood affects their work together, even though they can accurately identify the mood. Team moods are primarily created through emotional contagion, which is an unconscious tendency to mirror the body language and emotional tone of each other. Nonverbal cues and direct interpersonal contact are quite important in the transmission of emotional contagion in teams.

Team chemistry at its best is captured by the idea of "team spirit." The word *spirit* comes from the Latin *spiritus*, meaning "that force that gives life." It is closely related to spirituality because it is concerned with finding meaning and purpose in creative work to contribute something of value to the larger world.

CHEMISTRY AND BONDING

In terms of team chemistry, our research reveals that it is crucial to distinguish between "social" bonds and "work" bonds within a team. We once decided to use a ropes course to help build social bonds between members of a student team producing an original TV series. What we discovered was that, while the team developed strong social bonds, they became a barrier to developing meaningful work bonds because the members saw themselves as a happy family. This unintentionally created a barrier to creative abrasion, a necessary element of a highly functioning team.

It is our sense that developing a team for creative work requires a focus on developing what we term "work bonding."[7] Individuals generally enter into team environments with social bonding skills, but are usually as familiar with work bonding practices.

Effective collaboration and communication does not require that team members be social friends. We have found that starting with social bonding, more often than not, creates a false sense of harmony that suppresses divergent thinking, the expression of different perspectives, and postmortems necessary for creative work. It becomes a harmony facade and is the basis for more groupthink; different perspectives and ideas are withheld for fear of disrupting the social harmony. Social bonds may occur with some team members as they work on the creative project, but the primary focus should remain on the work bond.

Most research indicates that a diversity of experience, knowledge, and skills almost always precludes social friendships because those are more often than not based on similarity of thinking, interests, and beliefs. Work bonds are the basis for chemistry and authentic interdependence with a creative team.

Chapter Eleven

Commitment

"The relationship between commitment and doubt is by no means an antagonistic one. Commitment is healthiest when it's not without doubt but in spite of doubt."—Rollo May [1]

Doubt is a curious bedfellow of collaboration, not the least because it is always present and often warranted. But commitment in the face of doubt is a necessary attribute of success in teams. If there are any heroes on the team, then this commitment to effort is a cause they and their heroics can especially contribute to.

Commitment is a sincere and honest dedication to a team cause despite constant challenges and doubts. Like integrity, commitment is difficult to completely secure and control because it is most truly measured when no one is watching. It is the slow but sure exercise of collective conscience. Take this excerpt from a creative team member at the halfway point in a project:

> It seemed to me that no one on our team was deeply committed to our projects. You would notice that team members kept coming to meetings late. Sometimes they didn't show up, without letting anyone know they wouldn't be there. When we went into production, a number of team members would claim at the last minute that they couldn't help because there was some sort of emergency or they had previous plans that they couldn't possibly change.

While it might seem counterintuitive, creative abrasion within a team allows for the first significant level of commitment by team members. Contrary to popular belief, commitment in a creative team is not an all-or-nothing undertaking; rather, it is an evolving process.

Commitment among members of a creative team is a key component of what it means to be interdependent, to have to depend on each other as the project unfolds. But it does not happen instantly or uniformly or symmetrically. It happens in baby steps fueled by inspirational performances by key individuals.

Cascading commitment by all team members is quite crucial in a creative team's evolution. The old organizational model of commitment used to be along the line of, if team members are not capable of making a commitment, then they need to be removed from involvement with the team. Indeed, if someone is looking for an escape hatch or easy way out of work or exhibits insulting, bullying, and demeaning behavior, then there must be a quick parting of the ways. Though this is not always the rule, it is a very important element to establish. Additionally, for various reasons, not everyone is capable of working constructively in a team or meaningfully committing to a collective project. These members need to be quickly screened out to prevent a toxic effect on the team.

The evolving model of commitment is not a static one but rather a dynamic one of continual flux. It recognizes that all members of a team may not nor need not be expected to have 100 percent commitment, especially at the beginning of the creative project. However, the way the first team task is approached is quite important. In order for a creative team to work collaboratively, you need, at the very least, some level of commitment with constructive intent, which means a willingness to work things through with each other even though it is difficult. This could be considered a primitive materialization of the widely used rally call "All for one, one for all"[2] or the often-used rally call for teams: "**T**ogether **E**veryone **A**chieves **M**ore."[3]

Securing a commitment to an evolving project embedded with much uncertainty provides an opportunity for each team member to be creative in helping to construct and adding their personal touch to the project; that is, each member of the team needs to commit to finding a way to personally relate to the project that is meaningful and engaging for them. No team member can define this for another team member. When team members feel they have openly expressed their take on the creative project and have been though a constructive creative abrasion process with other team members, they are able to make an initial commitment to the project.

Constructive intent refers to team members' making the conscious decision to risk engaging themselves as fully as possible in the creative process by doing what they can to develop or improve the project. It is an aim that guides their action in working together. It is a commitment to being open to the collaborative process, the creative project, creative abrasion, and feedback in an uncertain journey together.

Team members who are more deeply committed to the team believe that the project is important and that team members need to show up, follow through, and stick with it even when the unfolding seems rough. As the level of commitment of team members grows, the level of collective creative energy also grows to produce an exceptional outcome. When levels of commitment deepen in a creative team, members find themselves energized and excited, and it becomes the backbone of the team.

Commitment provides a creative team with the strength to constructively work through difficult issues as they continue to evolve in their creative work together. As their level of engagement and commitment increases, they become more effective in influencing and comentoring each other and are less likely to get bogged down in discouragement—they never give up. They have the confidence and support to go through the most difficult times in their creative pursuits.

Team members collaborate at a higher level when they share a mutual, ever-deepening commitment to the project. Deepening team commitment fosters camaraderie, trust, and genuine caring for each other: all necessary to keep the team going over time.[4]

With commitment, as the team unfolds, members learn what they need to know to be more effective with each other. Team members also need time to try things, make mistakes, and then figure out what else they can do at a deeper level.

Commitment grows deeper when members

- Make decisions together
- Work through conflicts and divergent perspectives together
- Actively support one another
- Have fun and play together
- Overcome roadblocks together
- Hold each other to high standards
- Challenge each other to step up
- Express genuine appreciation of each other
- Actively learn from their errors and mistakes[5]

Commitment is the bedrock of a creative team or organization. It provides a creative team with its strength. Creative team members who are deeply committed tend to be the ones who don't take discouragement seriously; they don't give up. They set an example for those who don't have the confidence or experience to go through the difficult times and hold on to doing high-quality creative work together.

Creative team members tend to collaborate at a much higher level when they share commitment.[6] This is what a creative team needs to keep going in the long run. If people are committed to an effort for a period of time, then they will learn what they need to be more creative and effective. Commitment doesn't typically occur at only one moment of time.

While initial commitment is important, it can deepen or diminish within creative team members as the project evolves. It is more likely to deepen when team members support one another, work through divergent perspectives and personal conflicts, learn from mistakes and setbacks, remain vulnerable and open, and overcome obstacles. Commitment tends to diminish when the opposite occurs. When creative team members are not open and vulnerable and fail to support each other actively, the team will likely become engulfed in unresolved and undiscussed conflicts. Members of the team need to maintain focus on the commitment of the entire team to being vulnerable and actively supportive during the creative project.

Creative team members may vary in their level of commitment to the project at different times, and that is OK. It is important to appreciate whatever level of commitment a particular member can make. Some team members have more time, more interest in the project, and a deeper understanding of the value of working together. Team members need to feel their contributions matter even if they are small contributions. If they feel their efforts are devalued or dismissed, their commitment will likely wane.

Commitment to both the team and the creative project contains many unknowns and possibilities for failure. This is why vulnerability is crucial; the members of the team need to be able to openly express their doubts and fears. Most team members are quick to pick up on faked commitment. In expressing commitment, actions always speak louder than words.

Chapter Twelve

Empathy

"I think we all have empathy. We may not have enough courage to display it."—Maya Angelou[1]

Empathy in creative collaboration is like an artesian well. It's not too far below the surface, and if we can manage to break through to it, then it will open up a constant flow. Breaking through to empathy can be accomplished in everyday group interactions, from simple ice breakers to intense shared team experiences.

In our creative storytelling teams, we often see competition and ego at play between individual members. Recently, one such experience involved two students who had been placed in the role of director. As they moved into their roles, one assigned to direct the first episode and the other the second, they demonstrated distinctively different personality styles. Braden, a twenty-two-year-old white male, displayed an "alpha" personality, while Zhang Wei, a twenty-six-year-old Chinese student, displayed a more "beta" personality. Zhang Wei had been placed in the role of director of the first episode and was explaining his plans to visually capture a complicated scene involving extensive camera movement in a woodland setting. Braden challenged his decision and suggested an alternative strategy. Zhang Wei did not respond immediately, and an awkward silence ensued. "Why are you smiling?" Braden asked.

"I'm not really smiling," Zhang Wei replied. "I am nervous."

The whole room reacted in a wave of warmth, as if Zhang Wei had just articulated what everyone else was feeling—fear of letting his teammates down in his responsibilities. This is an example of empathy and emotional contagion—an expression of genuine feeling, opening up the opportunity for collective care. Empathy within a creative team is at its simplest just awareness of the emotions and feelings of other members as well as oneself. It is a connective link between individuals and other team members.

It can be divided into two components: affective empathy and cognitive empathy. Affective empathy consists of the feelings a team member experiences in response to the feelings of other members. It is the basis for emotional contagion within the team, where an unconscious emotional undercurrent instills the team with a particular emotional state. Cognitive empathy has to do with perspective taking, when a team member takes the perspective of other team members along with identifying his or her own emotions. Empathy is the opposite of apathy in a team. While empathy is understanding and sharing the feelings of others, apathy is a lack of interest, enthusiasm, or concern for others. Simply put, empathy at its root indicates that members of the team genuinely care for and engage with each other.

Creative teamwork is multidimensional, involving asking questions, providing honest critiques of the evolving project, seeking help, experimenting with new and untested actions, and seeking candid feedback. Engaged listening by team members is crucial in this process. Engaged listening must arise from team members' genuine curiosity to what other team members express. It is characterized by members making eye contact while focusing energy and attention on what the person is saying rather than figuring out what they want to say or evaluating what is being expressed. Additionally, it means team members pick up on feelings and the content of what is being expressed, including what is between the lines. They are aware of body language and nonverbal behavior.

Team members learn to summarize what other team members express and check to see if there is agreement. When asking for clarification or more details, team members use open-ended questions rather than yes-or-no questions. Additionally, each team member uses "I" statements to provide their reactions to what the other members have expressed. This means that emotions are also subjects for discussion between team members.[2]

Recent books on social-emotional intelligence, emotional intelligence, and empathy are testimony to the interest in learning how to identify and constructively handle emotions in ourselves and others as they occur in unfolding relationships. We prefer the term *emotional team skills* or *empathic team skills* to *emotional intelligence* or *emotional competence* because there is in everyone a capacity for learning to become aware of and identify emotions in themselves and others while also learning how to use the awareness constructively.

Much of the current research on emotional intelligence is abstract: Paper and pencil tests are used to measure a person's emotional intelligence, which is then correlated with team performance. The difficulty with this approach is that it does not examine how members of a creative team actually use emotions and feelings in their work together or how they have learned how to constructively use their emotions and feelings in a team. Similarly, there is scant research on how to develop emotional skills and empathy in a team.[3]

Team members need to either have or develop their interpersonal skills for regulating their emotional responses in difficult conversations with each other, especially when there are divergent viewpoints. This does not mean that team members need to take emotions out of the conversations; that is unrealistic and can lead to an emotionally explosive underground of hostility and negative back-biting. Denying and suppressing feelings is often much more destructive than letting them all spill out. All team members need to learn how to use their emotions with constructive intent to deepen their connection with each other. They need to develop the capacity for authentic empathy and realize they are not in competition with each other. Emotions experienced and expressed are often seen by nascent team members as potentially dangerous and therefore need to be avoided and controlled carefully so that they do not surface in relationships. Emotions that arise in working together, however, are not an illness; they are part of the human condition and tell us what matters most and what is really going on between us. They are important for team members to acknowledge. They are the heart and soul of what another member is experiencing within the team.

In withholding these emotional voices from one another, the team not only diminishes one another but they also dampen their ability to learn from one another about how to constructively use their emotions. Some team members may honestly say they feel nothing or they don't know what they feel. Typically, this means they have distanced themselves from their emotions. As a result, they have lost touch with learning how to identify and constructively use emotions in collaborating with others on the team.

Team members clearly identifying their emotions from moment to moment can be a daunting task. Research has identified four basic and fairly universal emotions: fear, sadness, anger, and joy. The language of emotions is a fuzzy one because there are so many ways to express them.

Each basic emotion can vary in intensity. For example, a team member can choose to label their experience of *anger* by describing it as feeling irritated, annoyed, pissed off, ticked off, or resentful. Anger is a sensation within us, while the words to describe it are outside us.

It is important that team members take responsibility for the feeling rather than attributing it to another team member.[4] Rather than saying to a team member "You make me angry when you . . ." a more effective statement is "I feel angry when you . . ." Team members take responsibility for their feeling when they use an "I" statements and do not couple it with such "you" statements as "You make me angry." The anger belongs to the team member experiencing it. Similarly, a statement like "You really hurt me" blames the other person for the hurt. The more effective response would be "I feel hurt."

It is a fact that we all have an inner emotional experience when we work together in a creative team. When we attempt to communicate our interpersonal experiences to one another, we search for words to describe them; often it is an imprecise, inexact, and ambiguous process. Language is simply a symbolic attempt to convey our inner experiences, which consist of sensations, intuitions, emotions, perceptions, and images that are not directly communicable. When the language we use evokes a similar inner experience in others, we are clearly communicating our own experiences. Yet we often know more of our experience than we can express through words. Much vicarious interpersonal and social learning happens in teams without the use of words, through social observation of the actions and nonverbal behavior of other team members.

There are few places in our culture where people can learn how to identify and constructively express their emotions in evolving relationships in creative teams. Members often feel that nonverbal behavior is not important or open for discussion. However, existing research indicates that a large portion of our communication with each other is nonverbal. Nonverbal behavior involves postures, facial expressions, eye gaze and movement, gestures, tone of voice, proxemics, haptics, and appearances. Facial expressions are what we see in the faces of others. Facial expressions for happiness, sadness, anger, and fear are similar globally. A smile, a frown, and a rolling of the eyes conveys much information on what others are experiencing in the moment. Gestures are bodily movements by others, such as waving, pointing, tapping feet, and crossing arms and legs. Tone of voice has to do with inflection (warm or cold tone), pitch, and volume. Whispering, for example, is quite different from shouting.[5]

Proxemics refers to the physical distances people prefer when relating to others. For example, during an intimate conversation with another person, one person may prefer twenty inches, while another might prefer four feet. Eye gaze refers to eye contact when speaking to other people and the look that it conveys, such as boredom, excitement, or engagement. Haptics refers to the ways touch is used or avoided in communicating with others. Touch can be used to communicate caring, encouragement, affection, control, and distance from another person.

Our cultural programing can prevent us from openly discussing either emotions or the body language that we observe and react to when we work together in a team. It is an unspoken norm that we assume is not appropriate or useful to bring into awareness and discussion. It is a silent taboo for relationships within teams.

Team members who have difficulty identifying their feelings sometimes are experiencing alexithymia. It is an ancient Greek word literally meaning "without words for emotions." These team members have trouble identifying the bodily sensations of emotional arousal or distinguishing between one feeling and another. This contributes to their detachment from themselves and makes it difficult for them to connect with other team members. They can, however, develop their personal skill in identifying feeling responses in themselves and other team members. Team members who have denied or blunted their feelings have typically not developed ways to constructively express them. Feelings to them are a secret, mysterious code.

Silent team members often say that they feel naked when they begin to express their emotions to the group. They feel awkward and uncomfortable. Several tools can enable team members to develop their feelings vocabulary.[6] In a sense, we are all prisoners of language in conveying our inner emotional experience. It is a tremendous relief to realize that language is a changing art form that we can use imaginatively to express our inner experiences. There are several ways that team members can express a particular experience in language to meaningfully relate to one another.

Being open to exploring ways of expressing themselves can be an exciting, engaging, and enriching learning experience. With practice and encouragement, team members can become more expressive while experiencing less stress in doing so. Learning to embrace people with a hug can be awkward at first, but with practice one develops a sense of spontaneity, stemming from the always fluid and evolving relationship.[7]

There are two primary social-emotional skills for team members:

1. an awareness of their own emotions and the ability to constructively express them
2. an awareness of other team members' emotions, along with the ability to acknowledge them [8]

The second skill category is often referred to as empathy, which includes the ability to use the awareness of others' emotions constructively to relate. It is also learning how to take the perspective of other team members. Additionally, it is helpful when learning to be constructively empathic to be aware of how interpersonal projection operates in relationships. [9]

Feeling either a strong positive or negative emotion when relating to a particular team member can inform us about our depths. It can provide a mirror into our unacknowledged selves and inner struggles. Team members who elicit intense attraction, admiration, repulsion, or fear usually indicate that we perceive something about them that we may have difficulty seeing and acknowledging in ourselves. When we are driven to not be like another team member, we often become the opposite.

When we don't own some part of ourselves, it goes underground and runs our lives. The emotional pain of our perceived flaws compels us to repress them and cover them up. We are all both worthy and worthless. Carl Jung believed that our unconscious first appears projected outside ourselves onto other people or objects. [10] Basically, we attribute to others things that are true about us that we may not be aware of.

Everyone projects their own attributes and feelings on to others. It is wired in. However, becoming aware of this natural process in a creative team provides useful insights into each member's own self. Denial and avoidance of projections increase defensiveness and diminish vitality and honesty with others and ourselves. When someone can acknowledge their projections, they decrease their defensiveness and increase their knowledge of themselves. Learning how to constructively deal with other team members' defenses as well as our own is vital to creative teams.

Projection or mirroring is one of the most common defenses in team relationships. This is an involuntary transfer of our own unconscious behavior to other team members so that it appears that these qualities exist in these team members rather than in ourselves. These qualities may be accurate for them, but it is also true about us. It is a defensive mechanism to diminish anxiety about unacceptable parts of ourselves. [11]

Interpersonal feedback between team members is an example of projection or mirroring in action. Being aware of what we project may be valuable for the person toward whom it is directed.

Mirroring is not simply a metaphor for a mental process. It is a physical process, as well. Scientist, who investigate nerve cells in the brain have discovered the physical basis of mirroring. They call these special brain cells "mirror neurons." These neurons are located in the part of the brain that controls thinking and action. They fire when we watch other people performing an action, resulting in us imprinting the action. Some scientist believe that mirror neurons are the physical source of empathy. We are hardwired to be emotionally reflective of others' feelings. Basically, in viewing other people, we can also see ourselves through the operation of mirror neurons.[12]

When we are able to openly acknowledge in our feedback what we mirror (e.g., "This is true about me and maybe it is true about you."), we constructively decrease interpersonal defensiveness and increase real learning between us. It requires vulnerability to constructively work through strong positive and negative emotions toward other team members.

The creative team needs to discuss emotion-laden issues with everyone present. Based on our experience, empathy is important for the lead manager to model when relating to members of the team. Leaders must also articulate what empathy is and why it is important for collaboration. Leaders who enact empathy with team members are likely the most powerful statement about its importance and the importance of genuine care. It is the key force in actuating real interdependence between team members.

Chapter Thirteen

Trust

"The way to make people trust-worthy is to trust them."—Ernest Hemming-way[1]

Trust is clearly a catch-22. How can we trust someone if we do not have evidence, experience, or guarantee that they can be trusted? This is exactly how the practice of trust begins in creative collaboration. However much we would like to say that a good team starts with trust, in reality a good team ends up with trust, borne out of risk, abrasion, and group action. Trust is a leap of faith at the beginning of collaboration, with the hope of realization at a later point in the process.

In astrophysical terms, trust is like the dark matter that surrounds celestial bodies in the universe. The vast majority of the universe is made up of the apparently empty darkness surrounding planets, galaxies, and black holes. The theory behind dark matter is that, contrary to its appearance, it is not empty but rather a vast form of matter and energy in the universe. If you think of a team as a universe and team members as celestial bodies, then trust is the invisible matter and energy surrounding them. Trust is intrinsic to the process of teamwork and, beyond that, a nutrient for team growth.

SYMBIOSIS OF FAILURE AND TRUST

When we talk to our students about the importance of trust, we begin with a discussion of failure. This is because the two are intrinsically entwined. As Ed Catmull explains, "Trust doesn't mean you trust that someone won't screw up. . . . It means you trust them even when they do screw up."[2] In this sense, earning trust is not a verdict. Instead it is a progressive process. Trust is built, not proven. When team members consider trust assurance with the possibility of their failure, their propensity to risk along with their propensity to produce and innovate explodes.

TRUST IN PRACTICE

Trust has long been considered a vital component for effective teamwork, even though its specific meaning is often vague. What does it really mean for members of a creative team to trust each other? How do you determine if there is trust among members of a creative team? How do you know that you can trust someone in doing a collective creative project? How do others know that they can trust you?

Trust doesn't magically happen by team members simply saying "I trust everybody." A state of trust exists in a creative team only when members expose their vulnerabilities, fears, failures, conflicting ideas, and emotions to the team as it evolves in its creative project. Only when these actions occur does a member believe that each member has a constructive intent to help others develop respectfully and constructively. They choose to be vulnerable and open with each other about their fears of working on the team, as well as their perceived limitations. They are open to asking for help and offering help to other members. They not only see themselves as co-mentors but also actually experience themselves as co-mentors to each other.

Vulnerability-based trust is a powerful, invisible force within a creative team that deepens the creative process and commitment of all members. It is a freeing and releasing process. Team members are free to focus their energy on creating and discovering with each other rather than on defending themselves. It releases their courage to experiment with new possibilities with each other. Vulnerability-based trust provides the freedom to explore and be open and creative. Members come to see each other with little defensive distortion and not as a threat but as companions and co-mentors in the adventure of the creative collaborative process. The open exposure of vulnerabilities, fears, and emotions by creative team members are indicative of a high trust level among them.

Trust is always fluid and evolving. It only evolves when creative team members risk being vulnerable and open in expressing their perspectives and feelings as the project unfolds. When it exists, members of the team feel safe to express themselves openly and freely because they experience the constructive intent of the team.

Trust-based vulnerability enhances the flow of the creative project. Creative energy is released and mobilized. All the creative processes of the team members are heightened. Both feelings and thoughts become more focused and energized. Team members act in more direct and effective ways with each other. As the adrenalin increases, the team itself transcends apparent limits, discovering new abilities of which they were previously unaware.

We have found that building trust on creative teams begins with members acknowledging their fears of failure and lack of constructive support from other members. One exercise we have used is, after team members have accepted a specific role for the project, other members face that member and say they trust them to perform the chosen role in an awesome manner. We than have the member who has agreed to take the role say, "And what if I fail or screw up?" The rest of the team members respond, "We will be there to help you." Highly creative teams are built on the cornerstone of vulnerability-based trust, collective engagement, and active collective support.

The two primary aspects of trust that significantly influence a team's creative output and work are the level of vulnerability and openness among members in what they are experiencing cognitively and emotionally in working together. When the trust level is high within in a team, the behavior of team members is more personal, open, creative, and interdependent. When the trust level is low, the behavior of team members becomes more impersonal, closed, indifferent, and either dependent (passive aggressive) or counter-dependent (rebellious). They display low commitment and either want to be spoon-fed or openly refuse to do anything outside their narrow role ("That is not my job"). Members also begin to arrive late, find excuses to not be there, leave early, feel the project is meaningless but don't voice it, and withdraw into themselves or blame the team itself for being a waste of their time.

In order for there to be meaningful creative ideas generated in collaborative efforts, there needs to be a strong level of trust and openness among team members. Many team members are not likely to express alternative points of view or different ideas if there is a fear of being shot down. Team members will hold back, hesitate, and shut down their creative or divergent thoughts. It can lead to unwillingness to make themselves vulnerable emotionally and intellectually.[3] Creating a culture of interpersonal safety within a creative team can help build trust.

Recent neuroscience research shows that our brains are hardwired to trust others.[4] Research shows that, in organizations that were perceived as having a higher trust level, team members were much more engaged at work, reported more energy and more output, had more empathy for other team members, felt closer to their team members, and reported a greater sense of accomplishment.[5]

The experience of being in a trusting environment also produces oxytocin. Otherwise known as the bonding hormone, the cuddle hormone, or the love hormone, it is released by the pituitary gland when people hug or bond socially and is responsible for human behaviors associated with relationships and bonding.[6]

Paul Zak and his colleagues conducted a series of studies to find out how the human brain determines when to trust someone.[7] They examined changing oxytocin levels of participants in a trust simulation created to ascertain their propensity to be trusting and trustworthy. They discovered that, when participants actually felt trusted by others, their brains produced more oxytocin. Additionally, with the rise in oxytocin, participants' behavior became more trustworthy.

They concluded that, when someone feels trusted, they actually become more trustworthy because of the increase in the oxytocin in their brain. He refers to this finding as the trust molecule. Once real trust begins to take hold in a creative team, it increases and reinforces itself.

For the manager working with a creative team, it is important to realize that trust does not develop to a crucial level until members have been vulnerable, engaged in creative abrasion, enacted psychological safety, and deepened commitment. When real trust exists in a creative team, there is an operating and energized interdependence among members.

Chapter Fourteen

Resilience

"She stood in the storm, and when the wind did not blow her away, she adjusted her sails."—Elizabeth Edwards[1]

P. H. Longstaff and Thomas Koslowski offer an applicable definition of *resilience* for the complex process of creative collaboration: "The capability to adapt and thrive. Resilience in social systems and psychology is often conceptualized as skill that an individual or group can bring to a disturbance that will allow it to reach a level of functionality that has been determined to be 'good.'"[2] Even though it is the last topic in the examination of effective collaboration, it is by no means the last process. It is a map for repeatable and sustainable success in teams, particularly in the face of great difficulty and adversity.

Disappointment is a fact of life. Resilience is an ineffable quality that allows team members to be knocked down by difficulties or failure and come back stronger than before. Rather than letting difficulties or failure overcome them and drain them, they find a way to rise above. Resilient team members are able to change course and move forward with renewed energy.

Resilience, then, is the ability of team members to remain productive and positive when faced with stress, uncertainty, and failure. They are able to cope or thrive with unexpected challenges. They have the passion and perseverance to move the creative project forward in a meaningful manner. Additionally, they develop the ability to cope with the ups and downs and bounce back from unexpected challenges. Resilience demands trust and maintains and improves the collaborative process going forward.

In our experiences, resilience is much easier to see once it blossoms than while it's growing. For instance, in late-phase meetings of highly functioning teams, members will genuinely look forward to feedback from their peers rather than dread it. Sometimes they will even demonstrate disappointment if they do not get sufficiently demanding or highly critical reviews of their work. This is a sign that their eyes are on results rather than personal gratification.

Resilience is powerful in molding a creative team. It entails four crucial processes: visibility, postmortems, team member interpersonal feedback, and mental mapping.

VISIBILITY

The Human Dynamics Lab at MIT under the supervision of Alex Pentland, Toshiba Professor of Media Arts and Sciences, has compiled findings on best practices for creative collaboration in teams.[3] In their research they developed an electronic smart ID badge along with SOE cell phone software that allowed them to measure how members interacted when working on projects. The smart electronic ID badges were fairly unobtrusive and noted such things as if team members faced one another; how much they talked, listened to each other, interrupted each other, and used gestures; the emotional tone of voice; and the level of empathic responding. In total, the electronic badges generated more than one hundred data points per minute. The researchers believed they were capturing natural team behavior after period of adjustment to the badges.

They examined 2,500 team members in twenty-one different types of organizations over a period of seven years for up to six weeks at a time. With the data collected, they were able to map out the communication patterns of members as they worked together and discovered a pattern that distinguished high-performing creative teams from less-effective teams.

The pattern had little variation, regardless of the type of team and its project (e.g., a call-center team striving for efficiency; an innovative team looking for a new product; a senior management group hoping to improve leadership). Creative high-performing teams had a clear data signature that was so powerful they were able to predict a team's performance simply by looking at the data from the electronic ID badges, without ever meeting the members of the team. All members of high-performing teams talked and listened about the same proportion of time throughout their projects. More specially, they talked and listened in equal measure. Team members' interactions were energetic, with a lot of face-to-face communication rather than e-mail and text. Fifty percent of the time, members talked together as a collectivity while; the other 50 percent of the time, they carried on side conversations with another team member. Lower-performing teams had dominant members, cliques within the team, and members who talked or listened but failed to do both.

The high-performing creative teams also engaged in frequent informal communications with each other about their project, even outside team meetings. They spent about half their time communicating outside of formal meetings or as "asides" during team meetings. These practices, rather than being seen as disruptions or annoying blocks actually increased opportunities for informal communication, support building, comentoring, and developing work bonding that increased team performance.

INVISIBILITY

In our recent work with a creative team, we discovered the following phenomenon we called an "invisible member" via total team feedback. This is what the "invisible member" learned from the feedback:

> I thought it was fine to be silent during our team meeting. I saw myself as not causing any trouble and contributing to the team in a supportive way from behind. However, after reading the feedback from team members, I found that the team members actually noticed and understood what was really going on with me.
>
> They knew from my body language and expressions that sometimes I disagreed and sometimes I had something to share even though I said nothing. They were ready to persuade me or support my opinions, but I didn't give them a chance to. Not giving others trouble is my philosophy. I thought keeping quiet would make me transparent and would not bother others. However, I found out the truth is, team members will be bothered much more when they know I have something to say, but I kept the words inside.

Overall, individual contributions and talents were less important than the communication pattern where everyone talked rather than just a few team members. There were no invisible or silent team members. Moreover, in the high-performing teams, any member felt free to talk to any other team member.

How team members communicate with each other turns out to be the most important predictor of team success and as important as all other factors combined including intelligence, personality, skill, and content of discussions. Pentland believes that these patterns of communication are highly trainable. He states,

> According to our data, it's as true for humans as for bees: How we communicate turns out to be the most important predictor of team success, and as important as all other factors combined, including intelligence, personality, skill, and content of discussions.
>
> The old adage that it's not what you say, but how you say it turns out to be mathematically correct.[4]

He goes on to suggest that these patterns of communications among team members are fairly easily learned.

These findings are quite similar to Google's findings on the important components of collaboration in creative teams. The findings of the Human Dynamics Lab are also quite consistent with the highly interdependent and creative organizational culture at Pixar and Disney.

POSTMORTEMS

It is in the postmortems and feedback that team members experience abrasion and discover that it is psychologically safe to be vulnerable and open with each other. This is the real guts of being an interdependent creative team.

There are multiple times as creative projects evolve that members of a team need to meet and honestly critique their work. While a postmortem is generally conducted at the end of the entire creative project, it is also useful at the end of each phase of a creative project. For example, in making a film or TV series, it is important to do a postmortem at the end of each short phase or shoot to improve performance in the next shoot. Taking the time to figure out what needs to improve and ways to improve the team's collective work process is well worth the time spent. This type of postmortem is about creative and intellectual ideas for improving the collective work of the team as it evolves in constructing something out of nothing.

A constructive postmortem requires candor, openness, and vulnerability among all members. Each member needs to be able to openly talk about mistakes and shortcomings of the project, as well as ways to overcome them and learn from them. It is here that moving away from the feeling of failure is important.

It is important throughout the creative process to ensure that each team member's concerns are heard and that they all feel they are owners of the project's success. They need to experience what they are doing as a truly synergistic creation. They realize in their experience that no one of them could have made their final project any better without their collective efforts.

Every team member needs a chance to openly share their reactions and comments, as all perceptions are equally valuable. Respectful and engaged listening by team members is a key factor in a constructive outcome. There are several ways a team postmortem can be constructively conducted. For example, each postmortem can start simply with team members discussing the following:

1. What went well?
2. What obstacles and difficulties did we experience?
3. What can we do differently next time to deal with the obstacles and difficulties?

The challenging part of a postmortem is constructively and openly discussing the difficult issues that arose in working together. Language and emotions are crucial here. Leading with a statement like "Allie acted unprofessionally by really screwing up lighting and sound" will most likely result in a stilted and defensive response. Using less demeaning language, such as "Allie is experiencing considerable difficulty in getting the lighting and sound the way it needs to be. Let's look at how this happened and what we can do to help her," can yield a better future performance.

The crucial thing in the postmortem is that team members focus on the obstacles and techniques to deal with them more effectively in the next shoot or rewrite. This is where team members can do much comentoring of each other and learn to ask for help and provide it to other members.

INTERPERSONAL TEAM MEMBER FEEDBACK

Feedback is helpful only when it is provided with constructive intent that indicates genuine concern for other members. There must be a willingness to comentor and actively support each other. Interpersonal task-oriented feedback is perceptual information about past behavior, delivered in the present, to influence future behavior, given by team members to each other in order to improve their creative collaboration.

Giving and receiving such perceptual feedback is not always an easy process.[5] Nevertheless, teamwork requires much feedback between members. It must be frequent and constant to meaningfully evolve the project. It is simply not enough to wait until the end of the project to share perceptual interpersonal feedback on someone's performance. There needs to be a continuous flow of performance feedback between the members of a creative team based on their specific roles in the collective work.

For this type of feedback to be useful, team members must be willing to be vulnerable in order to confront the reactions of other members to their performance on the team—ideally, without becoming defensive—as well as being willing themselves to provide honest feedback to other members. Stated somewhat differently, team members need to be willing to accept a critique of their work without thinking someone is attacking or criticizing them as a person.

Often this is not an easy process. It is another reason that establishing an interpersonally safe team culture is important. Often what keeps team members from providing each other with meaningful and honest perceptual feedback is the fear they will not be liked by other members or they will open themselves up to receiving negative feedback. Some fear of giving and receiving perceptual feedback stems mostly from inexperience in providing interpersonal feedback or negative past experiences in either giving or receiving feedback. It sometimes helps to realize we are all flawed, with considerable room to grow our talents. The idea of useful perceptual feedback is to build a supportive learning culture within the team while watching each other's back; it is not to fear someone sticking a knife into you.

All team members must realize that the feedback process is based on constructive intent to help them learn about their blind side (what others can see about them that they cannot see about themselves). At a minimum, for perceptual feedback to be constructive, it needs to be specific about the performance behavior and free of putdowns, insults, and slams. Compare the following examples of perceptual feedback given by one team member to another:

1. "I can't believe you spend all that time doing such shoddy lighting and sound. Don't you know any better?"

2. "The lighting and sound qualities are off. Let's take a look at what led to this."
3. "You are our team's motivator and compliment machine. I love how happy you are on set and how confident you are in our abilities. You make it a point to make everyone feel good about themselves and welcomed. You are a talented DP, and you a lot of knowledge about many different aspects of production. You tend to let Charlie run the show a bit too much, and I would like to see you trust your own eye."

The first comment is shaming, demeaning, and demotivating. The team member may feel putdown and confused about what they should do differently to handle the problem. The second and third comments are specific about the perceived performance behavior, so it takes the shame out of it while helping the team member gain information about what they can do to improve the lighting and sound problems.

Positive reinforcement certainly has its place in providing perceptual performance feedback, but to be constructive, it also needs to be specific and clear. Consider these two examples:

1. "Good job. Keep it up."
2. "Your writing was clear, your storylines were on target, and the writing was crisp and accurate. I particularly liked . . ."

The first comment may make a team member feel good, but it is so vague that the team member is not really sure what led to that conclusion. The team member might even feel discounted because the team member providing the feedback did not take time to mention what they actually did. In other words, a vague compliment seems canned and come across as lacking authenticity. The second comment is all positive about the perceived performance, but it tells a team member what is valued and indicates that the script was actually read.

Sometimes the most difficult feedback is not receiving any perceptual feedback from team members at all. When there is a lack of constructive intent, candor, and vulnerability in providing perceptual performance feedback, it is easy for a team member to feel that other members lack involvement or commitment to the creative project. There are cultural norms that often make asking other team members for perceptual feedback difficult. There are no rules against doing so but only those that are self-imposed. It is important that any team member feel free to ask for specific perceptual feedback from other members whenever they want. Crafting useful perceptual performance feedback to team members is a learned skill. It can be done poorly or extremely well. Explicitness in providing constructive perceptual performance feedback is not the same as providing tactlessness perceptual performance feedback.

Admittedly, it is easy to confuse interpretations of a team member's behavior with specific observations of their performance behavior. The provider of perceptual performance feedback has observations, although they more often than not also construct interpretations of the observed performance behavior. In providing perceptual performance feedback, it is helpful to tell the team member what you perceive or observe, the meaning you are assigning to the observation, how you feel about what you perceive, and if possible how you feel about that interpretation.

Sometimes it is helpful for team members to actually write feedback like an open, heartfelt letter to each member, including themselves. They indicate in their letters

1. how they personally experience the team member
2. what they see a particular team member constructively adding to the team
3. what they see the team member struggling with in the team
4. what specifically they would like the team member to explore in future work in the team

The team member writing the feedback signs their name so other team members can ask for clarification if they feel they need it.

Before the letters are distributed, each team member is asked to read through what they wrote and underline where the feedback is also valid for themselves. This is the way team members become aware of the projective nature of interpersonal project-oriented feedback.

We all project onto each other. It is not a sign of psychological pathology or a defense mechanism. It is part of our everyday perceptual process and the basis for empathy: What we focus on in other people is often what is also inside us, so we can tune into their feelings. In a sense, it takes one to know one.

It is not a matter of good or bad, right or wrong, but rather one of accurate or inaccurate. When team members grasp the projective nature of such feedback, it drastically changes the learning process from the feedback in an amazingly constructive manner. It is often powerful and quite moving for a team member to receive ten or more feedback letters written in this manner to experience how they are perceived by other members as they collaborate.

After each member has a chance to read the letters, the team assembles, and each member reports how they are experiencing their feedback and asks for clarification if they need it. At the same time, any other members who might be concerned with whether feedback was hurtful or off-base can check it out openly with the member in the spotlight. From our experience with this method of feedback, many members of the team feel validated by hearing what others see and value in them.

This form of feedback allows each team member to learn how they frame their experiences in the team through the language and words they choose. Moreover, it is not a forced set of statements created by someone else, nor is it a generalized checklist created by someone else. It comes straight from their hearts and minds. The members are also able to see how others frame their feedback, allowing them to learn how to provide more constructive and impactful feedback.

It is difficult to learn new ways of relating with vulnerability or interdependence without a model of constructive behavior. Team members present an array of effective and ineffective ways of dealing with vulnerability and interdependence. Through the process of mirroring, members will inculcate the modeled behavior into their repertoire of behavior with a team.

Team members as constructive models for other members is significant for the transformation from a singular mind-set to a collective mind-set. Acknowledging the constructive modeling aspects of team members can amplify the effectiveness of the interpersonal feedback process.

MENTAL MAPPING

Shared mental maps emerge as team members interact to make sense of their situation and cultivate shared beliefs about how they should work together to complete their creative task. Research indicates that shared mental maps among the members of a team is positively associated with both team processes and effectiveness.[6]

Shared mental maps refer to how team members conceptualize the process of creative collaboration. They indicate what they consider important and direct team members' behavior in working together. A constructive shared team mental map is rooted in recognition of team members' interdependence. It describes the creative team as evolving, connected, engaged interactions. The greater the connected, engaged interaction among team members, the greater the team's capacity to adapt effectively to needs and unexpected events.

When creative teams first come together, the most fundamental questions they face are "What are we really here for?" "What is our reason for being together?" and "How much autonomy and power do we really have?" Each team member brings to the team his or her own basic and often-unconscious assumptions. These influence the shared mental models that emerge to answer the team's questions.

Mental models are the team's shared, organized understanding and mental representation of knowledge about key elements of the operation. When team members have different areas of expertise, transactive memory functions as storage for expertise-allocation information and enhances the performance of teams by linking the different expertise domains.

A transactive memory system consists of the knowledge stored in each individual's memory combined with information pertaining to the different teammates' domains of expertise. The transactive memory system provides teammates with information regarding the knowledge they have access to within the team. Team members learn who knowledge experts are and how to access expertise through interactive communicative processes with other members. In this manner, a transactive memory system may provide team members with greater knowledge than any team member could access on their own.

Mental maps can provide a team with a sense of ownership over the process of creative collaboration. It can serve to strengthen feelings of engagement, responsibility, and influence over how the team approaches creative collaboration with each other. Research indicates that the feelings of ownership over the team's collaborative process facilitates creative collaboration, especially in teams whose roles and issues are continually evolving. A shared mental map involves the collective belief that all team members are responsible for and in charge of the team process itself. Team ownership of the collaborative process encourages team learning and development.

A shared team mental map should define effective creative collaboration as requiring continual learning supports and encouraging activities that advance the evolution of the collaborative process. Team members, when involved in the process of creative collaboration, expect each other both to seek outside knowledge and feedback and to share this with the team.

A potential barrier to learning in creative teams is admitting to a knowledge deficit or discussing developmental issues confronting the team, such as feedback to each other and mistakes. For example, if asking for help or feedback or discussing a failure or mistake is viewed as an interpersonal risk, then the willingness to seek learning opportunities is decreased. This clearly reflect the importance of creating a team culture that is experienced as interpersonal and psychological safe by team members.

A shared mental map supporting the need to learn must be anchored in a way that transcends perceived risk. Evolving team mental models are necessary for heedful relations among members of the team and in member interactions with individuals outside the team boundary. Interpersonal interactions assembled with heed are attentive, purposeful, conscientious, and considerate.[7] They increase team effectiveness by improving members' ability to work together efficiently. Without the enactment of heed, interpersonal interactions and relationships tend to be less than optimal.

Epilogue

Team Being

"We do not know how a butterfly works. We do not know how an egg becomes first a caterpillar, then a chrysalis, and then a butterfly—only that it does. Now and then we gain a little insight, but no more than you would of a hotel kitchen by looking in the doorway as the waiters pass in and out. At our present level of knowledge these developmental and behavioral processes may as well be magic, and therein lies the source of mystery, challenge, and excitement." [1]—Kjell Sandved and M. Emsley

Near the end of a creative team project, we often make a point of trying to catch the moment when the group of individuals we're working with turns into a team. The two are discernably different entities but so far impossible to witness in transformation—kind of like the moment the morning sun blazes over the horizon. Like the sun, a *true team* is either fully there or not there. This is the real meaning of team being.

METAMORPHOSIS

What does a true team look like? On the whole, the space they are in feels warm but not hot, particularly in the team members' nonverbal body signals. The energy level burns slowly, steadily, and positively. There is a laugh here and there, with a random sprinkling of both quiet and louder voices in reaction to developments. There is a crispness in what people say, and when they say it, they make consistent eye contact with each other. There is a spontaneity in interactions that wasn't there at the start—in short a room filled with candor.

Team members seem genuinely content being with each other. Every member of the team is engaged in some sort of activity connected to the project and are not waiting to be told what to do. There are several moving pieces of the project being attended to simultaneously yet not interfering with each other. There is a distinct feeling of coexistence. Though the deadline is near, members are clearly not panicked. They are energized.

When it happens—the transformation from a *ragtag group of individuals* to a *fully functioning team*—is, oddly, almost undetectable. The moment will pass without fanfare and usually escapes conscious identification. But it is there beyond a shadow of a doubt: a fittingly quiet metamorphosis. A creative team has emerged from its cocoon.

We have found the term *metamorphosis* useful for describing the first sign that a creative team has actually navigated the undercurrents to transforming from a singular mind-set to a collective, connected mindset. The word *metamorphosis* is from the Greek word for "transformation" or "transforming." There are, however, several definitions of the word. More generally, it is simply defined as a complete change of form, structure, or character. From a biological perspective, it is defined as a profound change in form or structure from one stage to the next in the life cycle of an organism, such as from a caterpillar to a pupa and from a pupa to an adult butterfly. It is remarkable: Looking at a caterpillar, it is unlikely that anyone could predict its emergence as a butterfly. As the saying goes, just when the caterpillar thinks it is dead, it turns into a butterfly and flies away. Likewise, we see a creative team emerge from a singular mind-set into a collective, connected mind-set, which announces that team being has begun.

Our experience in observing metamorphosis within creative teams indicates there are subtle but notable signs it has occurred. We see it happen as a team views the final product they have created together. For example, we have been with a large number of creative teams who collectively watch the film or TV series they have created. As they gather to watch it, there are notable signs of metamorphosis that signal their transformation from a singular mind-set to a collective, connected mind-set. There is a flowing spontaneity between the members rather than the hesitant interactions that existed at the beginning of the project. They make eye contact, and their nonverbals indicate an open, engaged connection with other members. They easily smile and laugh together while emitting much warmth. They are not afraid to touch and hug each other.

It seems like collectively they think, "Wow, we are truly a creative team. We created something together, and I like what we did. Could it be better? Yes, if we had more time, but I feel good about what we accomplished, and now I know from my experience how different people can create something together that we could not create by ourselves." They are in the true state of team being—realizing their creative power as a collective, connected mind-set.

In this book, we define the forces of creative collaboration that we have found must be addressed in developing a creative team. We describe the issues surrounding each of these forces, when team members step outside their self-imposed boxes and constructively open themselves to developing a connected mind-set. We do not articulate specific steps to handle each of the undercurrent forces. For example, we do not indicate specific steps to establish psychological safety in a creative team, nor does any research indicate what steps to take to establish it.

Our own experience is that, most importantly, members of a creative team must open themselves to feeling uncomfortable and together to stumble through issues they have brought into the team, such as not being vulnerable. No creative team has a clear, progressive order through the infinite possibilities. They only need to have a constructive intent and be open to learning by paying attention to what exists in them and their team as they evolve over time. The specific issues a team faces at any moment are and always will be unique to that team.

Based on years of experience, it is our belief that, if you want to learn how to be a collaborative team or manage one, then you need to take a risk and create such a team while committing to learning whatever transpires for vulnerability, conflict, and interdependence. There are no hidden rules or magical interventions to work your way through the undercurrents. Experience is the only reality; you cannot instruct anyone with just words to be effective in a creative collaborative team. You can only help them by designing learning situations with an ongoing team where they can examine their experiences and where the team learns through reflective self-awareness. The framework we develop here simply identifies in detail the consistent undercurrents that require navigating when the milieu of creative collaboration.

Learning new collaboration and teamwork skills is more effective when the learning process is active rather than passive. When a team member can take a theory, concept, or practice and try it on for size, they understand it more completely, integrate it more effectively with past learning, and retain it longer. They also learn to take interpersonal risks. Most of us believe more in knowledge we have discovered through our own experiences than we do in knowledge presented by others. Most concepts and theories are never really learned or wired-in until they are experienced and used.

While the experience itself is an important component of such learning, it needs to be anchored in a theoretical system that allows intellectual reflection to crystalize the learning in a cognitive manner. Thoughts, emotions, and actions tend to change as a whole rather than as separate parts. It takes more than information to change action theories, attitudes, and behavioral patterns. Just reading a book or listening to a lecture does not result in mastery of interpersonal, collaborative skills or team development. At best, they might generate interest in learning more about how to accomplish such changes. Action theories are steered by perceptions: perceptions of self, others, and the immediate situation affect how one feels, behaves, and believes. Changes in perception of self, others, and the team environment are necessary before changes in team action theories occur.

In this process, the greater the supportiveness of the team learning environment for exploring and risk taking, the greater the likelihood of risk taking, exploration, and trying on new behavior within the team. When the need for team members to defend and protect themselves diminishes, the likelihood of team members exploring new ways of thinking, emoting, and relating increases. It is clearly more effective to change any team member's action theory and behavior in the context of the team rather than in an individual-centered context.

It is necessary for the members to engage in effective, transforming teamwork processes for the team to be creative together. Once again, the types of teamwork processes necessary for effective creative team performance differ from most traditional conceptualizations of teamwork. In particular, the complexities of transdisciplinary problems require that, for the most effective creative problem solving to occur, team members must go beyond simple interaction among core participants in their particular specialty to integration of diverse and different perspectives from those with different specialties. Specifically, creative teamwork within this type of loose structure involves team members integrating their contributions for the best outcomes of the collective team.

In creative teams, this integration process is accompanied by a team transformation, where members are freed from singular specialty interests to collective team interests. Through this team transformation, members realize that they can most effectively accomplish their singular interests by developing a connected mind-set with other members. When this occurs, the members, at least temporarily, place the team's collective interests above their specific discipline self-interests, and team problem solving moves beyond narrow specialty concerns to a combined focus on interests of all discipline areas and how they relate to the creative project. It is this transformation focused on the connected mind-set over singular mind-set where the team members truly become committed team players—in essence they exist in a state of team being.

In creative transdisciplinary teams, where individual team members are able to integrate ideas across specialty areas and where team perspectives are placed above individual specialized perspectives, the potential for creative evolution is greatly enhanced. Rather than "creative" ideas being individually generated and guided by an individual's disciplinary perspective and self-interest, the idea-building process occurs freely and from a variety of perspectives; each team member, regardless of their role and skillset, builds on the best ideas of another. This is what the connected mind-set is all about.

Rather than a rigid, hierarchical structure, with each individual assigned certain roles where they are expected to remain, transdisciplinary team structures are more organic, with members often taking on different roles according to the team's changing needs. This type of creative teamwork is a transforming process, through which individual members break out of singularity and their own specialization areas to take on a collective perspective on evolving work issues; thus, they use the connected mind-set in their creative project, and in this process they become strongly committed and creative team players.

Within creative transdisciplinary project teams, members need to integrate information from each discipline, and the failure of a team member to contribute means a lack of representation of that member's role in the creative project. This could be devastating if the inadequate input results in a loss of potentially vital information.

Team members must work together to move out of their more narrowly defined specialty to approach problem solving from an integrative, collective perspective on the creative process. This involves developing the types of relationships within the team that allows each member to be open to and supportive of the suggestions of other members while not being fearful of creative abrasion.

Most importantly, however, transdisciplinary teamwork involves a team transformation to a connected mind-set, in which members of the team view themselves collectively as an interlocking set of members with evolving high-engagement roles. They have internalized the collective visions of the creative project and accepted this vision as the first priority for their work and the overall work of the team.

When a transformation takes place, a role-specific team, where the individual members are all in a singular mind-set, converts to one of a connected mind-set, with members taking risks and assuming additional activities outside of their roles as the project evolves to ensure that the best interests of the team are represented. Team members must venture out of their more secure discipline areas into situations where they may not be as sure of what they are doing and where their roles are not as well defined. Team members help each other to craft their fluid, emerging roles.

What we define as *role crafting* is an evolving concept flowing from interactions within the team. It requires greater effort on the part of the individuals and the team because it is more difficult to achieve an integration of many perspectives than it is for each member to focus solely on their own position and perspective; it requires them to think in new ways, to move from the singular mind-set to a connected mind-set, and to think outside the box.

The transformation to team being occurs when the members recognize that it is only through integration of inputs from multiple disciplines that they can achieve a truly more creative outcome than if they worked individually. For transdisciplinary project teams to achieve, they must wrestle with transformative processes at both the individual and team levels.

As the Zulus would say, explaining the meaning of *Ubuntu*, "Ubuntu Ngumuntu Ngabantu."[2] This simply means that a person is a person through other persons. South African Nobel laureate archbishop Desmond Tutu describes Ubuntu as "the essence of being human":

> It speaks of the fact that my humanity is caught up and is inextricably bound up in yours. I am human because I belong. It speaks about wholeness. It speaks about compassion.
>
> A person with Ubuntu is welcoming, hospitable, warm, and generous, willing to share. Such people are open and available to others, willing to be vulnerable, affirming of others, do not feel threatened that others are able and

good, for they have a proper self-assurance that comes from knowing that they belong in a greater whole.

They know that they are diminished when others are humiliated, diminished when others are oppressed, diminished when others are treated as if they were less than who they are. The quality of Ubuntu gives people resilience, enabling them to survive and emerge still human despite all efforts to dehumanize them.[3]

In exploring the complex forces at work in creative collaboration, we resist the temptation to reduce what we observe to simple steps for others to apply, however prone we may be to seek simplicity in our everyday lives. This is not to say that simple steps will not work. Our belief is simply that we see more agency, insight, and promise for creativity, innovation, and sustainability inside of the fiery complexities of creative collaboration. In some ways, like the butterflies that Sandved and Emsley describe, the behavioral processes involved in effective collaboration may as well be magic.

But if we free our minds, as David Bohm suggests, from the idea that order is always just some simple thing that we can grasp, then it isn't magic at all.[4] When we stare the complexities of teamwork in the face, it makes sense that our essence as individuals is enfolded in something much larger. Like water is to a crashing wave, we as human beings are to team being.

Notes

INTRODUCTION

1. Inbound, "Ed Catmull on His Definition of Creativity," YouTube, November 14, 2017, accessed February 17, 2019, https://www.youtube.com/watch?v=P_-Ba4RHJY8.

2. IBM Corporation, *Capitalizing on Complexity: Insights from the Global Chief Executive Officer Study* (Somers, NY: IBM Global Business Services, May 2010), accessed June 4, 2018, https://www-01.ibm.com/common/ssi/cgi-bin/ssialias?htmlfid=GBE03297USEN.

3. Peacefulness, "David Bohm Speaks about Wholeness and Fragmentation," YouTube, December 1, 2013, accessed February 23, 2019, https://www.youtube.com/watch?v=mDKB7GcHNac.

SINGULARITY

1. A. Stevenson (ed.), "Singularity," *Oxford Dictionary of English* (3rd ed.) (Oxford, UK: Oxford University Press, 2010), accessed July 5, 2017, http://www.oxfordreference.com/view/10.1093/acref/9780199571123.001.0001/acref-9780199571123.

2. Ibid.

3. A. Lightman, "What Came before the Big Bang? The Physics and Metaphysics of the Creation of the Universe," *Harper's Magazine*, January 2016, https://harpers.org/archive/2016/01/what-came-before-the-big-bang/.

1. A HERO'S QUANDARY

1. L. Gratton, "The Challenge of Scaling Soft Skills," *MIT Sloan Management Review*, August 6, 2018, https://sloanreview.mit.edu/article/the-challenge-of-scaling-soft-skills/.

2. R. C. Allen, "Engels' Pause: Technical Change, Capital Accumulation, and Inequality in the British Industrial Revolution," *Explorations in Economic History* 46, no. 4 (October 2009): 418–35, accessed December 31, 2018, https://www.nuff.ox.ac.uk/Users/Allen/engelspause.pdf.

3. J. Campbell, *The Hero with a Thousand Faces* (Princeton, NJ: Princeton University Press, 1949), 23.

4. World Economic Forum, *The Future of Jobs: Employment, Skills and Workforce Strategy for the Fourth Industrial Revolution* (Geneva: World Economic Forum, January 2016), http://www3.weforum.org/docs/WEF_FOJ_Executive_Summary_Jobs.pdf.

5. IBM Corporation, *Capitalizing on Complexity: Insights from the Global Chief Executive Officer Study* (Somers, NY: IBM Global Business Services, May 2010), accessed June 4, 2018, https://www-01.ibm.com/common/ssi/cgi-bin/ssialias?htmlfid=GBE03297USEN.

6. Quoted in J. Bersin, "New Research Shows Why Focus on Teams, Not Just Leaders, Is Key to Business Performance," *Forbes*, March 3, 2016, https://www.forbes.com/sites/joshbersin/2016/03/03/why-a-focus-on-teams-not-just-leaders-is-the-secret-to-business-performance/#37921e8924d5.

7. D. Agarwal, J. Bersin, G. Lahiri, J. Schwartz, and E. Volini, "Introduction: The Rise of the Social Enterprise," *2018 Global Human Capital Trends*, March 28, 2018, https://www2.deloitte.com/insights/us/en/focus/human-capital-trends/2018/introduction.html. For more on issues of individual mind-set in higher education and collaborative workplaces, see D. Ambrose, B. Sriraman, and K. M. Pierce (eds.), *A Critique of Creativity and Complexity: Deconstructing Clichés* (Rotterdam, Netherlands: Sense, 2014); E. E. Catmull, with A. Wallace, *Creativity, Inc.: Overcoming the Unseen Forces That Stand in the Way of True Inspiration* (Toronto: Random House, 2014); L. Curtin, "Quantum Leadership: Succeeding in Interesting Times," *Nurse Leader* 9, no. 1 (January–February 2011): 35–38; P. B. Paulus, "Groups, Teams, and Creativity: The Creative Potential of Idea-Generating Groups," *Applied Psychology: An International Review* 49, no. 2 (2000): 237–62; L. San Martín-Rodríguez, M.-D. Beaulieu, D. D'Amour, and M. Ferrada-Videla, "The Determinants of Successful Collaboration: A Review of Theoretical and Empirical Studies," *Journal of Interprofessional Care* 19, suppl. 1 (2005): 132–47; and B. Tabrizi, "75% of Cross-Functional Teams Are Dysfunctional," *Harvard Business Review*, June 23, 2015, accessed January 19, 2016, https://hbr.org/2015/06/75-of-cross-functional-teams-are-dysfunctional.

2. THINKING INSIDE THE BOX

1. D. Buckingham, "Introducing Identity," in *Youth, Identity, and Digital Media*, edited by D. Buckingham, the John D. and Catherine T. MacArthur Foundation Series on Digital Media and Learning (Cambridge, MA: MIT Press, 2008).

2. S. Atzeni and J. Meyer-ter-Vehn, "Nuclear Fusion Reactions," in *The Physics of Inertial Fusion: Beam Plasma Interaction, Hydrodynamics, Hot Dense Matter* (New York: Oxford University Press, 2004).

3. M. Iacoboni, *Mirroring People: The New Science of How We Connect with Others* (New York: Farrar, Straus, and Giroux, 2008); M. Iacoboni, "The Mirror Neuron Revolution: Explaining What Makes Humans Social," interview by J. Lehrer, *Scientific American*, July 1, 2008, https://www.scientificamerican.com/article/the-mirror-neuron-revolut/; and G. Rizzolatti and L. Craighero, "The Mirror-Neuron System," *Annual Review of Neuroscience* 27, no. 1 (2004): 169–92.

4. S. Milgram, *Obedience to Authority: An Experimental View* (New York: Harper and Row, 1974), 11; and M. Rodenbaugh and G. Gemmill, *Team Mirroring: Illusions and Realities of Team Dynamics and Development* (Doylestown, PA: Handley Group, 2004).

5. V. Gallese, M. N. Eagle, and P. Migone, "Intentional Attunement: Mirror Neurons and the Neural Underpinnings of Interpersonal Relations," *Journal of the American Psychoanalytic Association* 55, no. 1 (2007): 131–75; L. Graham, "The Neuroscience of Attachment," September 5, 2008, https://lindagraham-mft.net/the-neuroscience-of-attachment.

6. D. Eagleman, "'Incognito': What's Hiding in the Unconscious Mind," interview by T. Gross, *Fresh Air*, May 31, 2011, https://www.npr.org/2011/05/31/136495499/incognito-whats-hiding-in-the-unconscious-mind.

7. Milgram, *Obedience to Authority*.

8. Anando, "It's Now a Proven Fact—Your Unconscious Mind Is Running Your Life!" Lifetrainings, accessed August 18, 2019, http://www.lifetrainings.com/Your-unconscious-mind-is-running-you-life.html.

9. "Social Identity Wheel," Inclusive Teaching, August 16, 2017, accessed March 6, 2019, https://sites.lsa.umich.edu/inclusive-teaching/2017/08/16/social-identity-wheel/. For more on perspectives of individual dynamics in collaborative settings, see V. Gallese, "The 'Shared Manifold' Hypothesis: From Mirror Neurons to Empathy," *Journal of Consciousness Studies* 8, nos. 5–7 (2001): 33–50; G. Gemmill, "Managing the Dynamics of 'Having Nothing to Say' in Small Groups," in *The 2000 Annual*, no. 2 (2000), 206–11; G. Gemmill and G. Kraus, *A View from the Cosmic Mirror: Reflections of the Self in Everyday Life* (Bloomington, IN: Author-House, 2010); Rodenbaugh and Gemmill, *Team Mirroring*; and L. Winerman, "The Mind's Mirror," *Monitor on Psychology* 26, no. 9 (October 2005): 48–50.

VULNERABILITY

1. B. Brown, *Dare to Lead* (New York: Random House, 2018).

2. T. Laman, "Dance: And the Birds-of-Paradise," Bird Academy, 2013, https://academy.allaboutbirds.org/dance-and-the-birds-of-paradise/.

3. Ibid.

4. Brown, *Dare to Lead*.

5. D. Coyle, *The Culture Code: The Secrets of Highly Successful Groups* (New York: Random House, 2018). For more on vulnerability, see M. Schilpzand, D. M. Herold, and C. E. Shalley, "Members' Openness to Experience and Teams' Creative Performance," *Small Group Research* 41, no. 2 (December 2010): 55–76; and C. C. Finn, "Please Hear What I'm Not Saying," September 1966, https://poetrybycharlescfinn.com/pages/please-hear-what-im-not-saying.

3. UNCERTAINTY

1. M. J. Wheatley, *Leadership and the New Science: Learning about Organization from an Orderly Universe* (San Francisco: Berrett-Koehler, 1992).

2. E. E. Catmull, with A. Wallace, *Creativity, Inc.: Overcoming the Unseen Forces That Stand in the Way of True Inspiration* (Toronto: Random House, 2014).

3. M. Rabiger, *Directing: Film Techniques and Aesthetics* (Amsterdam: Focal Press, 2003).

4. W. Heisenberg, "The Physical Contents of Quantum Kinematics and Mechanics," translated by J. A. Wheeler and W. H. Zurek, in *Quantum Theory and Measurement* (pp. 62–84), edited by J. A. Wheeler and W. H. Zurek (Princeton, NJ: Princeton University Press, 1983).

5. D. Ambrose, B. Sriraman, and K. M. Pierce (eds.), *A Critique of Creativity and Complexity: Deconstructing Clichés* (Rotterdam, Netherlands: Sense, 2014).

6. Quoted in "What Life Means to Einstein: An Interview by George Sylvester Viereck," *Saturday Evening Post*, October 26, 1929.

7. D. S. Coffey, "Self-Organization, Complexity and Chaos: The New Biology for Medicine," *Nature Medicine* 4, no. 8 (1998): 882–85.

8. D. Coyle, *The Culture Code: The Secrets of Highly Successful Groups* (New York: Random House, 2018); and L. Curtin, "Quantum Leadership: Succeeding in Interesting Times," *Nurse Leader* 9, no. 1 (January–February 2011): 35–38.

9. L. San Martín-Rodríguez, M.-D. Beaulieu, D. D'Amour, and M. Ferrada-Videla, "The Determinants of Successful Collaboration: A Review of Theoretical and Empirical Studies," *Journal of Interprofessional Care* 19, suppl. 1 (May 2005): 132–47. For more on uncertainty, see R. K. Sawyer and S. DeZutter, "Distributed Creativity: How Collective Creations Emerge from Collaboration," *Psychology of Aesthetics, Creativity, and the Arts* 3, no. 2 (2009): 81–92; B. Tabrizi, "75% of Cross-Functional Teams Are Dysfunctional," *Harvard Business Review*, June 23, 2015, accessed January 19, 2016, https://hbr.org/2015/06/75-of-cross-functional-teams-are-dysfunctional; TED-Ed, "What Is the Heisenberg Uncertainty Principle?—Chad Orzel," September 16, 2014, accessed March 10, 2019, https://www.youtube.com/watch?v=TQKELOE9eY4; and A. W. Woolley, C. F. Chabris, A. Pentland, N. Hashmi, and T. W. Malone, "Evidence for a Collective Intelligence Factor in the Performance of Human Groups," *Science* 330, no. 6004 (October 29, 2010): 686–88.

4. FEAR

1. Franklin D. Roosevelt, inaugural presidential address, January 20, 1933,http://www.fdrlibrary.marist.edu/_resources/images/msf/msf00619.

2. H. S. Bracha, T. C. Ralston, J. M. Matsukawa, A. E. Williams, and A. S. Bracha, "Does 'Fight or Flight' Need Updating?" *Psychosomatics: Journal of Consultation and Liaison Psychiatry* 45, no. 5 (2004): 448–49.

3. S. E. Taylor, L. C. Klein, B. P. Lewis, T. L. Gruenewald, R. A. R. Gurung, and J. A. Updegraff, "Biobehavioral Responses to Stress in Females: Tend-and-Befriend, Not Fight-or-Flight," *Psychological Review* 107, no. 3 (2000): 411–29.

4. W. E. Deming, *Out of the Crisis* (Cambridge, MA: MIT Press, 2000).

5. A. C. Edmondson, "Managing the Risk of Learning: Psychological Safety in Work Teams," in *International Handbook of Organizational Teamwork and Cooperative Working* (pp. 255–75), edited by M. A. West, D. Tjosvold, and K. G. Smith (London: Blackwell, 2003); and A. C. Edmondson and Z. Lei, "Psychological Safety: The History, Renaissance, and Future of an Interpersonal Construct," *Annual Review of Organizational Psychology and Organizational Behavior* 1 (March 2014): 23–43.

6. A. Edmondson, "Psychological Safety and Learning Behavior in Work Teams," *Administrative Science Quarterly* 44, no. 2 (June 1999): 350–83.

7. See C. Duhigg, "What Google Learned from Its Quest to Build the Perfect Team," *New York Times Magazine*, February 25, 2016, https://www.nytimes.com/2016/02/28/magazine/what-google-learned-from-its-quest-to-build-the-perfect-team.html?smid=pl-share; J. Rozovsky, "The Five Keys to a Successful Google Team," re:Work, November 17, 2015, https://rework.withgoogle.com/blog/five-keys-to-a-successful-google-team/; and "Guide: Understand Team Effectiveness," re:Work, accessed August 18, 2019, https://rework.withgoogle.com/print/guides/5721312655835136/.

8. R. Kark and A. Carmeli, "Alive and Creating: The Mediating Role of Vitality and Aliveness in the Relationship between Psychological Safety and Creative Work Involvement," *Journal of Organizational Behavior* 30, no. 6 (August 2009): 785–804.

9. "Guide: Understand Team Effectiveness."

10. K. C. Kostopoulos and N. Bozionelos, "Team Exploratory and Exploitative Learning: Psychological Safety, Task Conflict, and Team Performance," *Group and Organization Management* 36, no. 3 (2011): 385–415.

11. E. R. Burris, J. R. Detert, and D. S. Chiaburu, "Quitting before Leaving: The Mediating Effects of Psychological Attachment and Detachment on Voice," *Journal of Applied Psychology* 93, no. 4 (July 2008): 912–22.

12. Edmondson and Lei, "Psychological Safety."

13. Edmondson, "Managing the Risk."

14. W. A. Kahn, "Meaningful Connections: Positive Relationships and Attachments at Work," in *Exploring Positive Relationships at Work: Building a Theoretical and Research Foundation* (pp. 189–206), edited by J. E. Dutton and B. R. Ragins (Mahwah, NJ: Lawrence Erlbaum Associates, 2007).

15. Edmondson, "Managing the Risk."

16. See Kahn, "Meaningful Connections"; and K. Leung, H. Deng, J. Wang, and F. Zhou, "Beyond Risk-Taking: Effects of Psychological Safety on Cooperative Goal Interdependence and Prosocial Behavior," *Group and Organization Management* 40, no. 1 (2015): 88–115. For more on psychological and interpersonal safety, see A. Idris, M. Dollard, and M. Tuckey, "Psychosocial Safety Climate as a Management Tool for Employee Engagement and Performance: A Multilevel Analysis," *International Journal of Stress Management* 22, no. 2 (2015): 183–206.

5. FAILURE

1. E. E. Catmull, with A. Wallace, *Creativity, Inc.: Overcoming the Unseen Forces That Stand in the Way of True Inspiration* (Toronto: Random House, 2014).

2. Ibid.

3. C. Abraham, and J. Gittell, "High-Quality Relationships, Psychological Safety, and Learning from Failures in Work Organizations," *Journal of Organizational Behavior* 30 (2009): 709–29.

4. P. Madsen, and V. Desai, "Failing to Learn? The Effects of Failure and Success on Organizational Learning in the Global Orbital Launch Vehicle Industry," *Academy of Management Journal* 52, no. 3 (2017): 451–76.

5. S. Cole, "'Fail again. Fail better.' Failure in the Creative Process," *Athens Journal of Humanities and Arts* 1, no. 3 (2014): 183–92; and B. Fletcher, "Want to Recover from Failure?

Then Feel the Pain, Says New Study," Netdoctor, September 18, 2017, https://www.netdoctor.co.uk/healthy-living/news/a28887/how-to-deal-with-failure.

6. Madsen and Desai, "Failing to Learn?"

7. G. Petsko, "Risky Business," *Genome Biology* 12, no. 6 (2011): 119. For more on failure, see University of Southern California, "Making a Mistake Can Be Rewarding, Study Finds," *Science Daily*, August 25, 2015, https://www.sciencedaily.com/releases/2015/08/150825103111.htm; and R. Sutton, "Learning from Success and Failure," *Harvard Business Review* (June 2007).

6. AUTHORITY

1. Ragni, "Steve Jobs Talks about Managing People," YouTube, June 12, 2010, accessed March 12, 2019, https://www.youtube.com/watch?v=f60dheI4ARg.

2. G. Gemmill, "The Dynamics of Scapegoating in Small Groups," *Small Group Behavior* 20, no. 4 (1989): 406–18.

3. C. Odom, "How to Lead with Influence Rather than Authority," Ladders, April 13, 2018, https://www.theladders.com/career-advice/author/curtis-l-odom, accessed 03/13/2019.

4. E. E. Catmull, with A. Wallace, *Creativity, Inc.: Overcoming the Unseen Forces That Stand in the Way of True Inspiration* (Toronto: Random House, 2014).

5. L. Curtin, "Quantum Leadership: Succeeding in Interesting Times," *Nurse Leader* 9, no. 1 (January–February 2011): 35–38.

6. G. Hamel, "First, Let's Fire All the Managers," *Harvard Business Review* (December 2011).

7. See Intuit, "Holacracy 101: Could This Nontraditional Business Structure Work for You?" December 28, 2016, https://quickbooks.intuit.com/r/structuring/holacracy-101-could-this-nontraditional-business-structure-work-for-you; and F. Laloux, *Reinventing Organizations* (Millis, MA: Nelson Parke, 2014).

8. D. Snierson, *Breaking Down* Breaking Bad (DVD), July 19, 2013.

9. S. Milgram, *Obedience to Authority* (New York: Harper and Row, 1974).

10. See G. Gemmill, "The Mythology of the Leader Role in Small Groups," *Small Group Behavior* 17, no. 1 (1986): 41–50; and G. Gemmill and J. Oakley, "Leadership: An Alienating Social Myth?" *Human Relations* 45, no. 2 (1992): 113–29. For more on authority, see C. Anderson and C. Brown, "The Functions and Dysfunctions of Hierarchy," *Research in Organizational Behavior* 30 (2010): 55–89; R. A. Barker, "The Nature of Leadership," *Human Relations* 54, no. 4 (April 1, 2001): 469–94; S. Denning, "Why Hierarchies Must Sign Their Own Death Warrant to Survive," *Forbes*, December 2, 2013, https://www.forbes.com/sites/stevedenning/2013/12/02/why-hierarchies-must-sign-their-own-death-warrant-to-survive; Gemmill, "Dynamics of Scapegoating"; and R. D. Hodge, "First, Let's Get Rid of All the Bosses," *New Republic*, October 4, 2015, https://newrepublic.com/article/122965/can-billion-dollar-corporation-zappos-be-self-organized.

7. DIFFERENCE

1. K. Kaye, *Workplace Wars and How to End Them: Turning Personal Conflicts into Productive Teamwork* (New York: American Management Association, 1994).

2. S. E. Page, *The Diversity Bonus: How Great Teams Pay Off in the Knowledge Economy* (Princeton, NJ: Princeton University Press, 2017).

3. Ibid.

4. S. Johnson, *Where Good Ideas Come From: The Natural History of Innovation* (New York: Penguin, 2011).

5. See Q. Roberson, O. Holmes, and J. Perry, "Transforming Research on Diversity and Firm Performance: A Dynamic Capabilities Perspective," *Academy of Management Annals* 11, no. 1 (2014); and Y. Solomon, "9 Diversity Factors That Will Increase Team Creativity," *Inc.*, May 25, 2016, https://www.inc.com/yoram-solomon/9-diversity-factors-that-will-increase-team-creativity.html.

6. See P. Dizikes, "Study: Workplace Diversity Can Help the Bottom Line," *MIT News*, October 7, 2014, accessed September 7, 2016, http://news.mit.edu/2014/workplace-diversity-can-help-bottom-line-1007; D. Fan, "Proof That Diversity Drives Innovation," August 31, 2011, http://www.diversityinc.com/diversity-management/proof-that-diversity-drives-innovation; and D. van Knippenberg, C. K. W. De Dreu, and A. C. Homan, "Work Group Diversity and Group Performance: An Integrative Model and Research Agenda," *Journal of Applied Psychology* 89, no. 6 (2004):1008–22.

7. M. Rigoglioso, "Diverse Backgrounds and Personalities Can Strengthen Groups," *Stanford Graduate School of Business*, August 1, 2006, accessed September 7, 2016, https://www.gsb.stanford.edu/insights/diverse-backgrounds-personalities-can-strengthen-groups; and S. Ellison and W. Mullin, "Diversity, Social Goods Provision, and Performance in the Firm," *Journal of Economics and Management Strategy* 23, no. 2 (2014): 465–81.

8. M. Misercola, "Higher Returns with Women in Decision-Making Positions," Credit Suisse, March 10, 2016, https://www.credit-suisse.com/about-us-news/en/articles/news-and-expertise/higher-returns-with-women-in-decision-making-positions-201610.html.

9. See Page, *Diversity Bonus*; K. Phillips, "How Diversity Makes Us Smarter," *Scientific American* (October 2014); and Rigoglioso, "Diverse Backgrounds and Personalities."

10. G. Gemmill and L. Schaible, "The Psychodynamics of Female/Male Role Differentiation within Small Groups," *Small Group Research* 22, no. 2 (1991): 220–39; and Johnson, *Where Good Ideas Come From*. For more on difference, see E. Deggans, "Hollywood Has a Major Diversity Problem, USC Study Finds," *The Two-Way*, February 22, 2016, https://www.npr.org/sections/thetwo-way/2016/02/22/467665890/hollywood-has-a-major-diversity-problem-usc-study-finds; C. Fernandes and J. Polzer, "Diversity in Groups," in *Emerging Trends in the Social and Behavioral Sciences*, edited by R. Scott and S. Kosslyn (New York: John Wiley and Sons, 2015); T. Kurtzberg, "Feeling Creative, Being Creative: An Empirical Study of Diversity and Creativity in Teams," *Creativity Research Journal* 17, no. 1 (2005): 51–65; E. Mannix and M. Neale, "What Differences Make a Difference? The Promise and Reality of Diverse Teams in Organizations," *Psychological Science in the Public Interest*, 6, no. 2 (2005): 31–55; K. Yeager and F. Nafukho, "Developing Diverse Teams to Improve Performance in the Organizational Setting," *European Journal of Training and Development* 36, no. 4 (2012): 388–401.

CONFLICT

1. See J. Farh, C. Lee, and C. Farh, "Task Conflict and Team Creativity: A Question of How Much and When," *Journal of Applied Psychology* 95, no. 6 (2010): 1173–80; C. Langfred and N. Moye, "Does Conflict Help or Hinder Creativity in Teams? An Examination of Conflict's Effects on Creative Processes and Creative Outcomes," *International Journal of Business and Management* 9, no. 6 (2014): 30–42; and E. Miron-Spektor and L. Argote, "Paradoxical Frames and Creative Sparks: Enhancing Individual Creativity through Conflict and Integration," *Organizational Behavior and Human Decision Processes* 116, no. 2 (2011): 229–40.

2. K. J. Behfar, R. S. Peterson, E. A. Mannix, and W. M. Trochim, "The Critical Role of Conflict Resolution in Teams: A Close Look at the Links between Conflict Type, Conflict Management Strategies, and Team Outcomes," *Journal of Applied Psychology* 93, no. 2 (2008): 462, doi: 10.1037/0021-9010.93.2.462; and B. Yingshan, Z. Fangwei, H. Yue, and C. Ning, "The Research on Interpersonal Conflict and Solution Strategies," *Psychology* 7, no. 4 (2016).

8. RISK

1. Victor Elias, *The Quest for Ascendant Quality* (Sparta, NJ: On QUEST, 2017), 167.

2. See J. K. Esser, "Alive and Well after 25 Years: A Review of Groupthink Research," *Organizational Behavior and Human Decision Processes* 73, nos. 2/3 (1998): 116–41; and I. L. Janis, *Victims of Groupthink: A Psychological Study of Foreign-Policy Decisions and Fiascoes* (Boston: Houghton Mifflin, 1972).

3. J. B. Harvey, *The Abilene Paradox and Other Meditations on Management* (Lexington, MA: Lexington Books, 1988).

4. Ibid.

5. M. B. Elmes and G. Gemmill, "The Psychodynamics of Mindlessness and Dissent in Small Groups," *Small Group Research* 21, no. 1 (1990): 28–44.

6. Nemeth, C., "The Value of Minority Dissent," in , *Minority Influence* (pp. 3–15), edited by S. Moscovici, A. Mucchi-Faina, and A. Maass (Nelson-Hall Publishers: Chicago, 1994).

7. S. Moscovici, E. Lage, and M. Naffrechoux, "Influence of a Consistent Minority on the Responses of a Majority in a Color Preparation Task," *Sociometry* 32 (1969): 365–79.

8. C. Nemeth, *In Defense of Troublemakers: The Power of Dissent in Life and Business* (New York: Basic Books, 2018).

9. K. Ronit and C. Abraham, "Alive and Creating: The Mediating Role of Vitality and Aliveness in the Relationship between Psychological Safety and Creative Work Involvement," *Journal of Organizational Behavior* 30, no. 6 (2009): 785–804. For more on risk, see S. Critchfield, "How to Push Your Team to Take Risks and Experiment," *Harvard Business Review* (March 2017); and M. A. Idris, M. Dollard, and M. Tuckey, Psychosocial Safety Climate as a Management Tool for Employee Engagement and Performance: A Multilevel Analysis," *International Journal of Stress Management* 22, no. 2 (2015): 183–206.

9. ABRASION

1. J. Hirshberg, *The Creative Priority: Driving Innovation in the Real World* (New York: Harper Business, 1998).

2. J. O'Toole and W. Bennis, "A Culture of Candor," *Harvard Business Review*, July 31, 2014.

3. Hirshberg, *Creative Priority*.

4. S. Glaze, "The Impact of Teamwork and Steve Jobs' Parable of Rocks," Great Results Team Building, November 25, 2014, https://greatresultsteambuilding.net/impact-teamwork-steve-jobs-parable-rocks/.

5. L. Hill, G. Brandeau, E. Truelove, and K. Lineback, *Collective Genius: The Art and Practice of Leading Innovation* (Boston: Harvard Business School, 2014), 130–34. For more on abrasion, see J. Farh, C. Lee, and C. Farh, "Task Conflict and Team Creativity: A Question of How Much and When," *Journal of Applied Psychology* 95, no. 6 (2010): 1173–80; D. Honan, "Why This Movie Doesn't Suck: The Culture of Dissent at Pixar Animation Studios," *Big Think*, December 12, 2011, http://bigthink.com/re-envision-toyota-blog/why-this-movie-doesnt-suck-the-culture-of-dissent-at-pixar-animation-studios; S. Kaufman, "How Convergent and Divergent Thinking Foster Creativity," *Psychology Today*, February 9, 2012, https://www.psychologytoday.com/us/blog/beautiful-minds/201202/how-convergent-and-divergent-thinking-foster-creativity; C. Langfred and N. Moye, "Does Conflict Help or Hinder Creativity in Teams? An Examination of Conflict's Effects on Creative Processes and Creative Outcomes," *International Journal of Business and Management* 9, no. 6 (2014): 30–42; M. Losada and E. Heaphy, "The Role of Positivity and Connectivity in the Performance of Business Teams," *American Behavioral Scientist* 47, no. 6 (2004): 740–65; E. Miron-Spektor and L. Argote, "Paradoxical Frames and Creative Sparks: Enhancing Individual Creativity through Conflict and Integration," *Organizational Behavior and Human Decision Processes* 116, no. 2 (2011): 229–40; and S. Moscovici, E. Lage, and M. Naffrechoux, "Influence of a Consistent Minority on the Responses of a Majority in a Color Preparation Task," *Sociometry* 32 (1969): 365–79.

INTERDEPENDENCE

1. K. Lewin, "When Facing Danger" (1939), in *Resolving Social Conflicts: Selected Papers on Group Dynamics* (pp. 159–68), edited by G. W. Lewin (New York: Harper and Row, 1948), 165.

2. E. N. Lorenz, "Atmospheric Predictability as Revealed by Naturally Occurring Analogues," *Journal of the Atmospheric Sciences* 26 (1969): 636–46, http://dx.doi.org/10.1175/1520-0469(1969)26‹636:APARBN›2.0.CO;2.

3. C. Teuscher and D. Hofstadter, *Alan Turing: Life and Legacy of a Great Thinker* (Berlin: Springer, 2004), 54. For more on interdependence, see Lewin, "When Facing Danger."

10. CHEMISTRY

1. S. Johnson, *Where Good Ideas Come From: The Natural History of Innovation* (New York: Penguin, 2011).
2. ABC News, "Coach K: A Winner's Mind," YouTube, June 8, 2010, accessed March 16, 2019, https://www.youtube.com/watch?v=smlewelwseQ.
3. Johnson, *Where Good Ideas Come From*.
4. "Guide: Understand Team Effectiveness," re:Work, accessed August 18, 2019, https://rework.withgoogle.com/print/guides/5721312655835136/.
5. C. Duhigg, "What Google Learned from Its Quest to Build the Perfect Team," *New York Times Magazine*, February 25, 2016, https://www.nytimes.com/2016/02/28/magazine/what-google-learned-from-its-quest-to-build-the-perfect-team.html?smid=pl-share.
6. Ibid.
7. L. Davey, "If Your Team Agrees on Everything, Working Together Is Pointless," *Harvard Business Review*, January 31, 2017, https://hbr.org/2017/01/if-your-team-agrees-on-everything-working-together-is-pointless.

11. COMMITMENT

1. R. May, *Courage to Create* (New York: W. W. Norton, 1995).
2. A. Dumas, *The Three Musketeers*, Project Gutenberg, November 27, 2016, https://www.gutenberg.org/files/1257/1257-h/1257-h.htm.
3. Author unknown.
4. See A. Neininger, N. Lehmann-Willenbrock, S. Kauffeld, and A. Henschel, "Effects of Team and Organizational Commitment: A Longitudinal Study," *Journal of Vocational Behavior* 76 (2010): 567–79; and C. Sheng, Y. Tian, and M. Chen, "Relationships among Teamwork Behavior, Trust, Perceived Team Support, and Team Commitment," *Social Behavior and Personality: An International Journal* 38, no. 10 (2010): 1297–1305.
5. C. Aube and V. Rousseau, "Team Goal Commitment and Team Effectiveness: The Role of Task Interdependence and Supportive Behaviors," *Group Dynamics: Theory, Research, and Practice* 9, no. 3 (2005): 189–204.
6. C. Agnew, "Commitment, Theories and Typologies," *Department of Psychological Sciences Faculty Publications*, paper 28, 2009, https://docs.lib.purdue.edu/cgi/viewcontent.cgi?article=1023&context=psychpubs; and N. Kokemuller, "The Effects of Team Commitment," Chron, 2019, http://smallbusiness.chron.com/effects-team-commitment-42028.html.

12. EMPATHY

1. M. Angelou, quoted in K. Murphy, "Maya Angelou," *New York Times*, April 20, 2013, https://www.nytimes.com/2013/04/21/opinion/sunday/a-chat-with-maya-angelou.html.
2. I. J. Hoever, D. van Knippenberg, W. P. van Ginkel, and H. G. Barkema, "Fostering Team Creativity: Perspective Taking as Key to Unlocking Diversity's Potential," *Journal of Applied Psychology* 97, no. 5 (2012): 982–96.

3. A. Feyerherm and C. Rice, "Emotional Intelligence and Team Performance: The Good, the Bad, and the Ugly," *International Journal of Organizational Analysis* 10, no. 4 (2002): 343–62.

4. G. Gemmill, "Managing the Dynamics of 'Having Nothing to Say' in Small Groups," *The 2000 Annual*, no. 2 (2000): 206–11.

5. Ibid.

6. See P. Allan, "Find the Perfect Word for Your Feelings with This Vocabulary Wheel," LifeHacker, October 30, 2014, https://lifehacker.com/find-the-perfect-word-for-your-feelings-with-this-vocab-1653013241; and University of California, Los Angeles, "Putting Feelings into Words Produces Therapeutic Effects in the Brain," *Science Daily*, June 22, 2007, https://www.sciencedaily.com/releases/2007/06/070622090727.htm.

7. Gemmill, "Managing the Dynamics."

8. J. D. Cox, "Emotional Intelligence and Its Role in Collaboration," *Proceedings of ASBBS* 18, no. 1 (2011): 435–45.

9. G. Gemmill and G. Kraus, *A View from the Cosmic Mirror: Reflections of the Self in Everyday Life* (Indianapolis: AuthorHouse, 2010).

10. C. G. Jung, "Archaic Man," in *Modern Man in Search of a Soul* (pp. 125–51) (New York: Harcourt, Brace, Jovanovich, 2017), first published in 1933.

11. Gemmill and Kraus, "View from the Cosmic Mirror."

12. Ibid. For more on empathy, see American Psychological Association, "Our Emotional Brains: Both Sides Process the Language of Feelings, with the Left Side Labeling the 'What' and the Right Side Processing the 'How,'" *Science Daily*, January 12, 2003, https://www.sciencedaily.com/releases/2003/01/030113072823.htm; H. K. Gujral, "Impact of Emotional Intelligence on Teamwork: A Comparative Study of Self-Managed and Cross Functional Teams," *International Journal of Multidisciplinary Research* 1, no. 6 (2011): 178; I. Kaur, C. Shri, and K. Mital, "Modelling Enhancement of Team Emotional Intelligence," *Journal of Business Perspective* 20, no. 3 (2016): 184–98; S. Long and J. Newton, "Educating the Gut: Socio-Emotional Aspects of the Learning Organization," *Journal of Management Development* 16, no. 4 (1997): 284–98; and D. H. Pink, *A Whole New Mind: Why Right-Brainers Will Rule the Future* (New York: Riverhead Books, 2012).

13. TRUST

1. E. Hemingway, *Ernest Hemingway, Selected Letters, 1917–1961*, edited by C. Baker (New York: Charles Scribner's, 1981), 23.

2. E. E. Catmull, with A. Wallace, *Creativity, Inc.: Overcoming the Unseen Forces That Stand in the Way of True Inspiration* (Toronto: Random House, 2014).

3. See A. Costa, R. Roe, and T. Taillieu, "Trust within Teams: The Relation with Performance Effectiveness," *European Journal of Work and Organizational Psychology* 10, no. 3 (2001): 225–44; and M. Hakanen and A. Soudunsaari, "Building Trust in High-Performing Teams," *Technology Innovation Management Review* (June 2012): 38–41, accessed August 3, 2016, http://timreview.ca/article/567.

4. C. Bergland, "The Neuroscience of Trust," *Psychology Today*, August 12, 2015, https://www.psychologytoday.com/blog/the-athletes-way/201508/the-neuroscience-trust.

5. See R. Adolph, "Trust in the Brain," *Nature Neuroscience* 5, no. 3 (2002): 192–93, doi: 10.1038/nn0302-192; J. Hills, "The Neuroscience of Trust . . . ," Head Heart Brain, February 6,

2016, https://www.headheartbrain.com/brain-savvy-hr/the-neuroscience-of-trust/; and P. J. Zak, *The Trust Factor: The Science of Creating High-Performance Companies* (New York: Amacom, 2017).

6. Hills, "Neuroscience of Trust."

7. Zak, *Trust Factor*. For more on trust, see C. Roussin, "Increasing Trust, Psychological Safety, and Team Performance through Dyadic Leadership Discovery," *Small Group Research* 39, no. 2 (2008): 224–48.

14. RESILIENCE

1. E. Edwards, *Resilience: Reflections on the Burdens and Gifts of Facing Life's Adversities* (New York: Broadway Books, 2010).

2. T. G. Koslowski and P. H. Longstaff, "Resilience Undefined: A Framework for Interdisciplinary Communication and Application to Real-World Problems," in *Disaster Management: Enabling Resilience* (pp. 3–20), edited by A. J. Masys, Lecture Notes in Social Networks series (New York: Springer, 2015).

3. See A. S. Pentland, "The New Science of Building Great Teams," *Harvard Business Review* 90, no. 4 (2012): 60–69; and A. Pentland, *Social Physics: How Good Ideas Spread: Lessons from a New Science* (New York: Penguin Press, 2014).

4. Pentland, *Social Physics*.

5. C. Seashore, E. Seashore, and G. Weinberg, *What Did You Say? The Art of Giving and Receiving Feedback* (North Attleboro, MA: Douglas Charles Press, 1992).

6. A. P. J. Ellis, "System Breakdown: The Role of Mental Models and Transactive Memory in the Relationship between Acute Stress and Team Performance," *Academy of Management Journal* 49, no. 3 (June 2006): 576–89.

7. K. E. Weick and K. H. Roberts, "Collective Mind in Organizations: Heedful Interrelating on Flight Decks," *Administrative Science Quarterly* 38 (1993): 357–81. For more on resilience, see V. Druskat and A. Pescosolido, "The Content of Effective Teamwork Mental Models in Self-Managing Teams: Ownership, Learning and Heedful Interrelating," *Human Relations* 55, no. 3 (2002): 283–314; R. Klimoski and S. Mohammed, "Team Mental Model: Construct or Metaphor?" *Journal of Management* 20, no. 2 (1994): 403–32; E. Michinov and J. Juhel, "Multilevel Influences of Team Identification and Transactive Memory on Team Effectiveness," *Team Performance Management* 24, nos. 1–2 (2018): 106–20; and R. Oertes and C. Antoni, "Phase-Specific Relationships between Team Learning Processes and Transactive Memory Development," *European Journal of Work and Organizational Psychology* 24, no. 5 (2015): 726–41.

EPILOGUE

1. M. Emsley, *Butterfly Magic*, photographs by K. B. Sandved (London: Pelham, 1975).

2. S. C. Lundin and B. Nelson, *Ubuntu! An Inspiring Story about an African Tradition of Teamwork and Cooperation* (New York: Broadway Books, 2010).

3. D. Tutu, quoted in TempletonPrize, "Who We Are: Human Uniqueness and the African Spirit of Ubuntu," April 3, 2013, https://youtu.be/0wZtfqZ271w.

4. D. Bohm, quoted in Peacefulness, "David Bohm Speaks about Wholeness and Fragmentation," December 1, 2013, accessed February 23, 2019, https://www.youtube.com/watch?v=mDKB7GcHNac.

About the Authors

Gary Gemmill, PhD, is professor emeritus of organizational behavior at Syracuse University, where he instructs, consults, and does research on the psychodynamics of working together in collaborative creative teams. He also has a global consulting practice dealing with collaborative leadership and leadership development.

Michael Schoonmaker, PhD, is professor and chairman of the Television-Radio-Film Department at Syracuse University's Newhouse School. He is the author or co-author of three previous books: *Educating the Post-TV Generation, Unlocking the Moviemaking Mind*; and *Making Television Programs*. His professional credits include managing roles in production with MTV and NBC.

Made in the USA
Columbia, SC
29 August 2020